D0970511

DISTINGUISHED COMPANY

Sir John Gielgud

DISTINGUISHED COMPANY

Doubleday & Company, Inc.
Garden City, New York
1973

BY THE SAME AUTHOR:

Early Stages
Stage Directions

Excerpts from tribute to Vivien Leigh which appears in
Vivien Leigh: A Bouquet by Alan Dent. Reprinted by
permission of Hamish Hamilton, Ltd.

ISBN: 0-385-04563-8
Library of Congress Catalog Card Number 72–96237
Copyright © 1972, 1973 by John Gielgud
All Rights Reserved
Printed in the United States of America
First Edition in the United States of America

To JAMES DALE

whose charming book *Pulling Faces for a Living*
gave me the notion of attempting to set down
some of my own youthful theatrical enthusiasms

ACKNOWLEDGEMENTS

I would like to thank Mander and Mitchenson for their invaluable help in choosing the illustrations from their Theatre Collection, and for reading the proofs.

Sir Cecil Beaton was kind enough to find for me amongst his collection pictures of Lady Cunard and Lady Colefax.

FOREWORD

I had the remarkable good luck to be born into a great theatrical family, the Terrys, on my mother's side.

My father, of Lithuanian origin, was also of distinguished theatrical ancestry, although I never heard him boast of it.

So I was born, if not with a silver spoon in my mouth, in the equivalent of a rich theatrical dress basket.

Though both my parents loved the theatre, neither of them had any wish to act themselves, and they taught their children (my two brothers, my sister, and myself) to look upon going to the play as a special kind of treat, something of an occasion to be saved up for, looked forward to, and discussed afterwards in fascinating retrospect.

I must have had more persistence than I realized at the time to persuade them that they should allow me to become a professional actor.

In my childhood, boyhood, and adolescence I was not only stagestruck, but obsessed by the fascination of the many great theatrical personalities of the day, memories which have obstinately remained most vividly with me ever since.

When I was a boy and a young man I had the privilege of working with some of the players of whom I have written in this book, as well as knowing many of them in private life. I hope I have not belittled their talents or their quality by repeating anecdotes about them which are occasionally trivial or absurd. I have always loved listening to older players as they told of their past experiences, and cherished my own favourite stories and recollections. I have tried to sort out some of these youthful enthusiasms and to recall them as accurately as I can, without embroidery or fabrications, while I still remember them so vividly over so many years.

CONTENTS

FOREWORD   *v*

LIST OF PLATES   *xi*

1   *Overture—Beginners*   *1*

    CHU CHIN CHOW

    THE SHAKESPEARE TERCENTENARY

2   *Family Portrait*   *15*

    FRED, MARION, AND DAME ELLEN TERRY

3   *Brother and Sister*   29

    EDWARD AND EDITH GORDON CRAIG

4   *Three Witty Ladies*   43

    MRS. PATRICK CAMPBELL

    LADY TREE

    DAME LILIAN BRAITHWAITE

5   *New York*   61

        PAULINE LORD
        JOHN BARRYMORE
        JANE COWL
        LESLIE HOWARD
        VIVIEN LEIGH

6   *Some Non-Acting Actors*   75

        SIR CHARLES HAWTREY
        ALLAN AYNESWORTH
        GERALD DU MAURIER
        RONALD SQUIRE
        A. E. MATTHEWS

7   *Two Splendid Character Actresses*   85

        ADA KING
        HAIDÉE WRIGHT

8   *Three Brilliant Eccentrics*   95

        ESMÉ PERCY
        ERNEST THESIGER
        ROBERT FARQUHARSON

9   *Two Exquisite Comediennes*   105

        DAME MARIE TEMPEST
        YVONNE ARNAUD

10   *Three Great Character Actors*   *117*

      LESLIE FABER

      SIR CEDRIC HARDWICKE

      CHARLES LAUGHTON

11   *A Brilliant Leading Lady*   *129*

      GERTRUDE LAWRENCE

12   *Two Forceful Actors*   *135*

      ROBERT LORAINE

      CLAUDE RAINS

13   *Remarkable Hostesses*   *143*

      LADY COLEFAX

      LADY CUNARD

14   *Music Halls*   *153*

15   *Down to Earth*   *163*

      INDEX   *171*

LIST OF PLATES

Frontispiece: the author as a boy

following page 12

Edward Gordon Craig, 1956
Ellen Terry and Edith Craig in *Henry VIII*, 1892
Marion Terry with A. E. Matthews in *Peter's Mother*, 1906
Fred Terry

following page 36

Jane Cowl
John Barrymore as Hamlet
Lilian Braithwaite, 1908
Vivien Leigh

following page 60

Lady Tree, 1935
Mrs. Patrick Campbell, 1913
Gerald du Maurier in *Interference*, 1927
Charles Hawtrey in *Ambrose Applejohn's Adventure*, 1921
Toni Edgar Bruce, Lottie Venne, Leon Quartermaine, Allan Aynesworth and E. Holman Clark in *The Circle*, 1921

following page 84

Haidée Wright in *Milestones,* 1912
Haidée Wright and Robert Lorraine in *The Father,*
   1927
Ada King in *The Queen Was in the Parlour,* 1926
Ernest Thesiger and Sybil Thorndike in *Saint Joan,*
   1924
Robert Farquharson in *The Cenci,* 1922

following page 108

Esmé Percy with his last dog, Skippo
Marie Tempest, 1906
Ronald Squire, Yvonne Arnaud, and Leslie Faber in
   By Candle Light, 1928
Cedric Hardwicke and Gwen Ffrangcon-Davies in
   The Barretts of Wimpole Street, 1930

following page 132

Cronin Wilson, Charles Laughton, and Ben Weldon
   in *On the Spot,* 1930
Noël Coward and Gertrude Lawrence in *Private Lives,*
   1930
Lady Cunard, *c.* 1935

following page 156

Lady Colefax with Rex Whistler, *c.* 1937
Claude Rains, John Gielgud, Felix Aylmer, and
   Tristan Rawson in *Robert E. Lee,* 1923

1

OVERTURE—BEGINNERS

My first play—*Peter Pan—The Boy Who Wouldn't Grow Up*.
I must have been seven years old at least when I saw him first.
(Actually he was born the same year that I was, in 1904.)
Pauline Chase played Peter, Hilda Trevelyan was Wendy, and
Holman Clark was Hook. There was a drop curtain painted
to look like a huge sampler, and a mysterious character called
Liza who ran across at the beginning and was supposed to
have written the play. I was thrilled by the first entrance of the
Pirates, drawn on a kind of trolley with Hook enthroned at
the centre of the group, and the sinister song that heralded
them as they approached from behind the scenes. I loved
Nana taking the socks in her mouth from the nursery fender.
Was she a real St. Bernard, I wondered, or a man dressed up
and walking on all fours? But I resented the wires on the
children's backs which I could see glittering in the blue limelight, and guessed that their nightgowns had bunched-up ma-

terial on the shoulders to hide the harness they wore underneath. And I wished the wallpaper at the top of the scenery
didn't have to split open, as well as the tall windows, when
the time came for them to fly away. Trap doors immediately
fascinated me—the one in *Peter Pan,* through which the little
house rose slowly at the end of the play, with Peter and
Wendy waving to the audience from its windows, and the one
in *Where the Rainbow Ends* which suddenly whisked the
wicked Aunt and Uncle to the nether regions. And of course
I loved the fights in both plays: Peter and Hook, St. George
and the Dragon King, and the double scene above and below
ground in *Peter,* and the hollow tree with stairs inside it, with
Hook in a green limelight leaning over the low door at the
bottom, leering at the children as they lay asleep.

I never much cared for pantomimes. The story was always
so disjointed, and the Principal Boy who was a girl, the Dame
who was a man, and the knockabout comedians and topical
songs, made the whole thing very confusing and difficult for
me to follow.

These are early memories, of course—childhood treats
when my grandmother or my parents always accompanied
me. But later in my school days, with a latchkey in my pocket
and a few half-crowns carefully saved up from my allowance,
I would spend long impatient hours waiting in a queue for
the pit or gallery of a theatre, with my brother Val or a school-
fellow for company. After our long hours of waiting we
would hear the doors being unbarred at last and would shuf-
fle slowly along in line to pay our money.

In those days the strange method of admission was not by
paper ticket but by a metal disc, which was shovelled out from
the booking-window after we had paid our shilling or half-
crown. Then, clutching our disc, we had to drop it back into
the slit of a wooden box a few yards farther on before we

were finally admitted. We rushed along a dark passage to a flight of steep steps leading down to the pit, or climbed several long flights of stone stairs to reach the gallery. The seats, when we clambered into them at last, were hard wooden benches, sometimes with iron back-rests, sometimes without, so that the knees of the people sitting in the row behind us would press sharply against our shoulders. As we looked down from the gallery the floor of the stage looked absurdly raked, and the actors at the back of a scene were often only visible from the waist downwards, while from the pit our view of the stage was often blocked by tall people sitting in the stalls and by late-comers pushing past them to reach their seats.

In some theatres the underside of the dress circle hung very low, and from the pit the top of the proscenium was cut off completely, and there were often pillars which one had to dodge in order to see the stage at all. If the play was a great success extra rows of stalls would be added and the pit reduced to a few rows at the very back of the theatre, while the second balcony (the "upper" circle as it was called in those days) was often enlarged during a successful run, and the gallery pushed back till it consisted of only a few seats close up against the roof.

Advertisements, bills, and programmes were designed individually, and I always connected certain colours and type-setting with various managements and their respective theatres. His Majesty's used buff colour, with red and black print in very bold readable lettering, and the Haymarket, Wyndham's, and the St. James's all had their own particular types of bills. Then there were boards outside the theatre which displayed only one name, known, when I learned theatrical jargon, as "double-crowns." On these bills the name of each star in the play would be printed singly (as well as in lights, along with the title of the piece, over the main entrance), but a few of the principal supporting players would also be featured on individual boards, and when an actor began to be cast in more important parts he would look forward to the moment when the management might think him sufficiently important to merit one all to himself.

Shaftesbury Avenue, Charing Cross Road, and St. Martin's Lane looked much as they do today, though one no longer sees tramps and down-and-outs sleeping on newspapers in the alleys at the back of the theatres. But Soho (with its three-course meals in the little restaurants for a shilling or two) was still like a discreet foreign village, and the clutter of cheapjack advertisements, reeking food counters and shoddy porn shops, were not to disfigure the neighbourhood for many years to come. Charing Cross Road was filled with respectable second-hand book shops, and the less discreet "rubber shops" did not begin till you had passed the Palace Theatre on your way to the Tottenham Court Road.

The Café Royal was still one of the sights of the West End, frequented by a crowd of painters and Bohemians. The main brasserie was approached by a long ramp leading from the front doors in Regent Street past a big kiosk selling foreign papers and magazines, and my eldest brother took me there one day in 1915, when he was on leave, and pointed out Augustus John holding court, with his earrings, red beard, and wide black felt hat. On the following afternoon we went together in a box to the Alhambra to see *The Bing Boys on Broadway* (arriving, to my dismay, nearly half an hour late for the performance after a festive lunch party at the Gobelins Restaurant in Rupert Street where I had sat fidgeting and agonizingly looking at my watch). George Robey leaned over the footlights and picked up one of my chocolates, grinning and raising his huge black eyebrows, and Violet Loraine sang one of her songs, as I thought, looking especially in my direction. How did I react, I wonder, to this early experience of audience participation? Fascinated, perhaps, but a bit alarmed as well.

First nights in London used to be such great occasions—at least I thought so. The queues would begin to form outside the theatre several hours earlier than usual, though they behaved in a more orderly fashion than in Victorian days (as my father used to describe them to me) when the men had to move their ladies into the centre of the crush, and protect them by shoving with their elbows in the stampede that always took place as soon as the doors were opened. My father first admired my mother, before he ever met her, when he saw her from the Lyceum pit as she sat with her mother and sisters in a box at one of Irving's first nights.

I came to recognize many of the habitual first-nighters—the critics, including A. B. Walkley of *The Times* and Malcolm Watson of the *Morning Post,* Edward Marsh, with his pointed jutting eyebrows and a monocle, Willie Clarkson, the wig maker, Courtenay Thorpe the actor, with a frilled shirt and false white-gloved hand, quizzing the house through a gold lorgnette, and Mrs. Aria, who had been Irving's last devoted friend and was a famous wit. ("In all matters pertaining to Sir Henry," she once observed to a young lady who repeated some indiscreet gossip at a party, "I believe I am considered to be the past-mistress.") Various leading actors and actresses—one of the Vanbrugh sisters perhaps, Marie Tempest, or even Ellen Terry, were quickly recognized as they entered the stalls or boxes (they timed their appearances with care so as not to divide the interest of the pit and gallery) and would be greeted with excited cries and enthusiastic applause which they would acknowledge gracefully, bowing to the audience as they took their seats. The curtain would rise at least ten minutes late, and there would be more excitement as the scenery (also applauded if it was at all spectacular) was disclosed, and more clapping as each of the principal actors made their entrance. In the intervals I looked forward to the buzz of argument and comment in the foyer and, at the end of the performance, the shouts of approval (or perhaps booing) from the gallery, and speeches from the star, the director (dragged on and usually ineptly inaudible) and sometimes from the author (whom the audience often failed to recognize). Then, after it was all over, the long journey back to South Kensington by tube or bus, dead tired but still arguing excitably all the way.

CHU CHIN CHOW

The year is 1916, and His Majesty's Theatre is packed with uniforms. I am twelve years old, sitting with my parents in my favourite seat, the middle of the front row of the dress circle. The lights go slowly down and music plays. Clouds of delicious incense are wafted from the stage as the gold fringed red velvet curtain rises on a dazzling palace scene, a dark blue banqueting hall with marble steps and a frieze of peacocks that looks like beaten gold. Negro slaves, led by a major domo in a huge turban carrying a wand, parade with covered dishes. "Here be oysters stewed in honey," they sing, "All for our great Lord Kassim." Oscar Asche makes his entrance, huge and impressive, with long moustaches and gilded fingernails, rattling his Chinese fan, and Lily Brayton, his wife, in a great wig of frizzled black hair, swathed in veils and jewels and transparent gauzes.

Courtice Pounds as Ali Baba, singing (with Aileen

D'Orme) the hit song of the evening "Any Time's Kissing Time." Sydney Fairbrother* as Ali Baba's comic wife Mahbubah. Frank Cochrane, as Kassim Baba, murdered in a cave full of jewels at the end of the second act, reappears in the part of a blind cobbler in the third. "And as I cobble with needle and thread, I judge the world by the way they tread." There are two real donkeys, several goats, some sheep, and at least one camel. The next time I come to see the play again—I shall see it nearly a dozen times—I shall have the added pleasure of watching the animals arriving at the dock-door as I stand waiting in the long queue, listening to the buskers and exchanging theatre gossip with my neighbours.

Chu Chin Chow ran for years (2,238 performances) but it always seemed fresh and fascinating to me, even when a dreaded slip in the programme would announce that one of my favourite players was ill or taking a holiday. But the lighting and scenery appeared as beautiful as ever, and a bill announcing "New scenes, New songs, New costumes," issued after two years' run, sent me scurrying off to His Majesty's once more. The piece was nothing in itself, simply the old fairy tale of *Ali Baba and the Forty Thieves,* but Asche had made it into a brilliant fantasy, part pantomime, part romance, part musical comedy, and had also written the book with the composer Frederic Norton, whose music was so charming and so hugely popular. Black velvet Moorish shutters (a kind of false proscenium) slid together at the end of each full scene, and opened to reveal insets on little rostrums where duets were sung while another full scene was prepared

---

* A brilliant eccentric actress—she was apt at rehearsal to produce live mice from her sleeves or bosom—adored dogs—and wore very strange clothes. "Don't care for jewellery, dear," she said to me once—"Beads can't resist them!"

behind, an infinitely more attractive solution than the flapping front cloths which had always been accepted before this time in plays demanding elaborate scenery.

Besides an excellent cast of players and a most convincing group of extras drilled to perfection, Asche had taken care to engage a number of beautiful girls, whom he deployed in the slave-market scene wearing spectacular and scanty costumes, a kind of London version of the Folies Bergères. This episode was naturally one of the production's most popular features, especially to the men on leave who crowded the theatre. Sir Herbert Tree, who had built His Majesty's, returned from America, where he had gone to recoup some past failures, to find his "Beautiful Theatre" packed to the doors with *Chu Chin Chow* and sat among the audience murmuring sadly, "More navel than millinery." In 1917 *Chu Chin Chow* opened in New York at the Manhattan Opera House where it ran for 208 performances.

It was in the same year that I saw the revue, *Vanity Fair*, produced by Alfred Butt at the Palace Theatre. The opening scene was set in Piccadilly Circus, and Arthur Playfair and Nelson Keys, two brilliant comedians, acted in a hilarious skit called "Two-chinned-chow"—Playfair imitating Oscar Asche, while Nelson Keys, in an enormous fuzzy wig, with bare legs, his arms covered with bracelets and hands spread out with palms downwards in Cleopatra style, ran coyly round the Eros fountain, his body swathed in black wrappings with two large yellow hands embroidered on them, appearing to clasp him round the waist. He gave a brilliant caricature of Lily Brayton's way of talking in the play, with a lot of pseudo-Oriental jabber, and the scene ended with the Forty Thieves entering from the back of the stage, carrying on their shoulders the sandwich-boards which were commonly used to advertise plays in the streets in those days. The boards were

printed in large letters in the colour and type of the posters
for His Majesty's, and read, "Stalls Full," "Dress Circle Full,"
"Gallery Full," "Awfull."

SHAKESPEARE TERCENTENARY PERFORMANCE
2 MAY 1916

Drury Lane Theatre, a gala matinée

My brother Val and I sit with our parents, in the Upper
Circle this time, as seats for such a grand occasion are very
expensive. King George and Queen Mary arrive in the Royal
Box and the whole audience rises to greet them. Sir George
Alexander has arranged the performance, as Tree (considered to be the leader of the Profession) is still in America.
The programme is a formidably long one, nearly half an hour
of orchestral pieces and some solos by various eminent singers,
followed by the whole of Shakespeare's *Julius Caesar,* and a
pageant to finish up with, as well as speeches from Sir Squire
Bancroft and Mrs. Kendal. But of course we sit spellbound
from beginning to end. The Forum scene is magnificently
played, with a great crowd of distinguished citizens led by
Gerald du Maurier and Edmund Gwenn. We quickly decide
that Henry Ainley, stripped to a leopard skin for the games
in the opening scene, is an ideal Mark Antony, and Arthur
Bourchier a rather dull and heavy Brutus. Also that Cassius,
superbly played by H. B. Irving, is the best part in the play,
an opinion from which I have never wavered since. The
Alma-Tadema scenery, designed for Tree's production at His
Majesty's years before, is used again, with solid-looking pal-
aces, balconies and awnings, pillars, perspectives, and blue
skies.

During one of the intervals we hear a great outburst of

cheering from behind the curtain, and someone comes out to
tell us that Frank Benson, who is playing Caesar, has just
been sent for to the Royal Box, still in his corpse-like make-up
as the Ghost, to be knighted by the King with a sword hastily
borrowed from Simmonds, the theatrical costumier's round
the corner in King Street. The audience cheer wildly at the
announcement, taking up the applause from the huge crowd
of delighted players behind the scenes.

The great pantomime was still being presented every year
at Drury Lane by Arthur Collins, an experienced master of
such productions, and the previous Christmas he had used a
massive pillared set for the finale—wide steps stretching from
under the stage close to the footlights from the open trap,
rising to the very top of the huge stage, with two broad
landings to divide the ascending flights of stairs. The same
set is used again for the Shakespearean pageant this May
afternoon. Groups of characters from nine or ten of the plays
emerge in procession, coming up from below with their
backs towards the audience. On reaching the landings they
turn and reveal themselves—Ellen and Marion Terry as Portia
and Nerissa, Fred Terry and Julia Neilson as Benedick and
Beatrice, and dozens more. Every star of the legitimate and
musical stage in London at the time is recognized and greeted
by the enraptured house. The clapping never seems to stop.
When all the players in the various tableaux have been applauded and have stepped aside, curtains on the top landing
are drawn back, revealing a bust of Shakespeare on a plinth.
Flanking the bust are the figures of Comedy and Tragedy—
Ellen Terry in white and Geneviève Ward in black—and the
huge cast of players begin to move slowly up the last flight of
stairs to lay wreaths at the foot of the plinth. Finally with the
singing of the National Anthem, the curtain falls and the
performance is over.

He influenced the theatre all over the world even though the productions he achieved were very few. He hardly ever came back to England after leaving it at an early age, and died in Venice at the age of ninety-four. He was made a Companion of Honour in his last years, but this belated tribute to his genius from his own country came too late for him to take much pleasure in it, just as his illustrious mother, who had only been made a Dame of the British Empire in her declining years, was too old and infirm to enjoy the honour by the time she received it.

Craig's numerous amours in Europe caused considerable scandal over the years—especially his love affair with Isadora Duncan, the American dancer, whose child by Craig was tragically drowned in a car accident in Paris.

Edward Gordon Craig, 1956

Ellen Terry, whose own marriages and love affairs had brought her little happiness, adored her son and spent a great deal of her hard-earned savings in helping to support him and his numerous children—most of them illegitimate—as well as the women with whom he was associated at different times.

Edward Godwin, Craig's father, had never married Ellen, and no doubt the son inherited some of the father's weaknesses and was always resentful of his own illegitimacy.

In his last years he lived quite near Picasso and Somerset Maugham in the South of France, but he was not on visiting terms with either of them, though he did agree to give some radio talks with Max Beerbohm, an old friend who was also living in the neighborhood.

He told me, rather acidly, not to bother to go and see the Matisse Chapel, though, of course, I did. "Maugham?" he said. "No, I meet him sometimes in the bank. He has a magnificent motorcar waiting for him outside, but he never offers me a lift."

Ellen Terry as Queen Katherine and Edith Craig as her Lady-in-Waiting
in *Henry VIII* at the Lyceum Theatre, 1892

Ellen Terry once wrote: "When people speak of me after my death, I hope they will say I was a useful actress!"

Max Beerbohm called her "The incarnation of our capricious English sunlight."

The public, and many of her critics too, were fond of referring to her as a "great dear," but she resented the implication as a slur on her untiring industry and technical skill.

Henry James, who saw her act in London in the 1870s, was one of her few detractors. He found her "interesting but freakishly Gothic," and failed to understand her popularity and that of her sister Marion. But in her long and triumphant partnership with Henry Irving she was the best loved actress not only in England but also in America where she toured with Irving for several triumphant seasons.

Growing up under the shadow of her fascinating mother Edith Craig found it difficult to develop her own considerable talents, first as an actress, and later as a costume designer and an original stage director.

Marion Terry with A. E. Matthews in
Peter's Mother at Wyndham's
Theatre, 1906

A skilful and elegant actress with a beautiful low speaking voice that could break into tearful melting tones in an emotional scene, she was also a mistress of light comedy and farce.

My mother used to describe her to me waltzing with infinite grace in the old Manchester Town Hall, on a dance floor that was swung on carriage springs, and told me how, in a farce, *Engaged* by W. S. Gilbert, she made a dramatic entrance, somewhat disheveled after a railway accident. A large plate of buns stood on the table, and Marion, suddenly catching sight of them, sank into a chair and proceeded to devour the buns one after another with a rapturous expression on her face.

Fred Terry

He was something of a Victorian prude and had little sense of humour, but also a broad Rabelaisian streak which he endeavored to restrain except in strictly masculine company.

After a long and exasperating rehearsal of a scene in *Henry of Navarre*—a costume melodrama in which he was attempting to drill a raucous crowd of extras to convey the offstage horrors of the massacre of St. Bartholomew—the company, at the evening performance which followed, worked hard to satisfy the instructions of their chief.

As the curtain fell, Fred Terry turned to his beautiful wife, standing beside him, resplendently attired as Marguerite de Valois. "Julia," he ordered sternly, "go to your dressing room." As she obediently turned and left the stage, Fred strode to the back of the scene, and flinging open the canvas windows with a magnificent flourish, shouted, "Gentlemen! I could fart louder than that!"

Percy Macquoid, the great furniture and costume expert, who was also an experienced man of the theatre and had helped Tree and Alexander in many of their finest productions, was a great friend of my parents. He told us afterwards some funny stories of the great occasion. How Evelyn Millard, who played Calpurnia, begged, "Oh, Mr. Macquoid, couldn't I have a different togo?" and that Bourchier, when Macquoid remonstrated with him for wearing white socks with his sandals, looked very cross and demanded, "Ain't they right, old boy?" Geneviève Ward (who had played Queen Eleanor in *Becket* at the Lyceum with Henry Irving) was evidently something of a terror, and had made a fuss at being asked to share a dressing-room with a number of other distinguished actresses, not having bothered to read the imposing list of names pinned to the door. Ellen Terry, who was already in the room, making up quietly in a corner, was heard to murmur softly, "You always were a cat, Ginny!"

Miss Ward was, however, a fine tragedian, a famous Volumnia in *Coriolanus,* a part she often played with Benson's company, and the first actress to be made a Dame for her services to the stage. But Ellen Terry was not similarly honoured till several years later, presumably because of her marital irregularities, and the title only came to her when she was too old to take much pleasure from it. The whole theatrical profession was deeply indignant that she had not been the first actress to be singled out. As the two actresses stood opposite to one another at Drury Lane that afternoon, I remember watching Ellen Terry, as she held the mask of Comedy for many minutes in her outstretched hand, restlessly dropping it to her side from time to time, while Geneviève Ward stood like the Rock of Gibraltar, holding her Tragic mask with a grip of steel.

2

FAMILY PORTRAIT

FRED, MARION, AND DAME ELLEN TERRY

"Ladies and gentlemen. If there is anything an actor values more than your applause, it is your silent attention to detail which enables us to give you of our best. On behalf of my dear comrade Julia Neilson and all the comrades of my company, I thank you from my heart." This was one of Fred Terry's characteristic curtain speeches.

He was an imposing figure, my great-uncle, when I first became aware of him at my parents' Christmas parties, built on generous lines, with fine hands and red curly hair. Extremely shortsighted, and wearing gold pince-nez like his master, Henry Irving, he behaved, as he acted, in the grand manner, jingling the sovereigns in the pockets of his striped grey trousers—worn with a black stock, tailcoat, and button boots—the typical Edwardian actor-manager.

He loved his work with a dedicated devotion, and was touchingly sincere and simple in his attitude towards it. For him heroes and heroines were always white and villains always black. A faithful disciple of Irving, Tree, and Alexander, in whose companies he had so often appeared in his first years as a young actor, he followed their example by embellishing his own productions with fine scenery and lavish costumes, and drilled his crowds and ensemble scenes with loving care, perfecting elaborately worked-up entrances and effective "curtains" and using music to give background to dramatic or sentimental scenes. Max Beerbohm, writing of his performance in a drama entitled *Dorothy o' the Hall* (in which Dorothy Vernon danced with Queen Elizabeth), remarked, "Mr. Terry . . . hiding behind a bower of roses, thrust his face through the flowers, in sight of the audience, without seeming ridiculous. Mr. Terry thrusts his face thus and stays thus, for several seconds: and yet manages to remain, as he would say, 'mahnly.' It is a remarkable achievement."

Jolly, warm, and generous, he was also a man of violent prejudices, and subject to sudden and violent fits of apoplectic rage which quickly passed like clouds before the sun. His language could be sulphurous, though he managed to restrain it in front of ladies, to whom he was always extremely courteous. He was fond of gambling, and would spend long hours playing bridge at one of his London clubs (he was a great clubman) or swearing furiously if he played badly on the golf course or backed a loser on the race-course. On one occasion, feeling it was necessary to call a young actor to order for using bad language in the Green Room Club, he sent for the young man in question and spoke to him severely. "Well," said the culprit, "I seem to remember, sir, that I have sometimes heard you use fairly strong language in the Club yourself." "God all bloody mighty," retorted Fred Terry, "I'm the f . . . President."

He believed completely in the romantic nonsense in which

he acted so successfully, but in modern clothes he knew he could not achieve the splendid panache which so delighted his audiences when he was in period costume. He knew just how to swing a cape, flourish a feathered hat, sweep a magnificent bow, dance a minuet, spit his opponent with a flash of his rapier, or light up a commonplace scene with his lively presence and ringing laugh. But he thought Ibsen decadent and Shaw discursive. Clean, full-blooded romantic melodrama was his acknowledged field, and he revelled in it all through his theatre life, and occasionally in his private life as well.

Marion, his favourite sister, who acted so delightfully in plays by Wilde and Barrie, had also been beautifully trained in Shakespeare and costume plays. She too was somewhat narrow in her outlook and lacked humour in private life, where she demanded a good deal of flattery and attention. But she was a brilliant actress, shrewd enough to adapt her technique to a more realistic manner as time went by, even succeeding (as Lilian Braithwaite, who had often worked with her, when she herself was an *ingénue,* was also to do in *The Vortex* by Noël Coward some twenty years later) as "the woman with the past," when she created the part of the adventuress, Mrs. Erlynne, in Wilde's *Lady Windermere's Fan.* Her last appearance in London was in Somerset Maugham's *Our Betters,* as the Princess, one of the only two respectable characters in the comedy, which was considered at that time (1923) to be extremely daring, and I always wondered what Marion herself must have thought of the play when she agreed to act in it. Fred would most certainly have disapproved of it profoundly.

It is sad that Ellen Terry, the greatest and most famous of the Terry family, could not succeed in finding vehicles for her talent after leaving the Lyceum, whereas her sister and brother —Fred was the youngest of the family—continued to appear in London and the provinces right up to the Twenties. Ellen was to triumph only once more for a season at His Majesty's as Mistress Page with Tree (though Irving was still alive), in his Coronation production of *The Merry Wives of Windsor* in 1902. In this she appeared with Mrs. Kendal, her life-long rival and, according to my father, the best actress in England, though never to be compared in popularity with Ellen Terry. In 1905 Tree also presented *The Winter's Tale* for Ellen at his theatre though he did not himself appear in it (Charles Warner was Leontes), but she seems not to have made any great impression as Hermione. Her memory, as with all the Terrys, was treacherously uncertain, and her concentration easily disturbed, though she continued to the end of her life to enchant the public whenever they were lucky enough to see her on or off the stage.

Ellen Terry drew her characters, with instinctive genius, in broad strokes and generous flowing lines, but she seemed too restless to be confined within the walls of drawing-room comedy or even in contemporary heroic drama. Her failure as Hiordis in Ibsen's *The Vikings* (which she daringly produced in 1903 under her own management chiefly to display the scenic talents of her son Gordon Craig) must have made her wary of venturing into more experimental work. She had listened too late to Shaw's entreaties, and stayed too long at the Lyceum, with its fading fortunes, out of a strong sense of professional discipline and unwillingness to dissolve her long and triumphant partnership with Irving.

She could not help loving to be loved, and, as the public always preferred her to make them laugh or cry (they would have none of her as a tragedienne, either as Lady Macbeth or Volumnia), she went on playing Goldsmith's Olivia and Nance Oldfield,* with Portia and Katharine of Aragon to

---

* *Olivia* by Wills adapted from *The Vicar of Wakefield*. *Nance Old-field*, a one-act play by Charles Reade.

bring her back to her beloved Shakespeare from time to time, so long as the passing years allowed. In her seventies, when I heard her give her Shakespeare lecture readings, she could still give radiant glimpses of her former glory, and one could understand the older generation of playgoers who said, "She speaks Shakespeare as if she had just been talking to him in the next room." But the only two contemporary plays in which she appeared at the turn of the century, Barrie's *Alice Sit by the Fire* (1905) and Shaw's *Captain Brassbound's Conversion* (1906), proved something of a disappointment, and her divine gifts of tears and sunshine never seemed to inspire a new playwright to provide her with adequate material.

I think both Fred and Marion were always somewhat afraid of their elder sister, perhaps because she was apt to be slyly amused at their immense seriousness and respectability, and was basically far simpler and more unashamedly Bohemian than they were. When she was engaged by Doris Keane in 1919 to play the Nurse in *Romeo and Juliet*—her last professional appearance in a London run—she wrote with glee, "I am keeping all the rude bits in!"—a remark which would certainly have shocked her brother and sister. But perhaps the shade of Irving would have chuckled. Himself a somewhat bitter and ironic humorist, he had never been able to resist her enormous sense of fun, even when she arrived late for rehearsals and broke up the other actors by fooling during a performance, behaviour which he would never have countenanced from anyone else within the sacred portals of his theatre.

All the Terrys had healthy appetites, enormous courage, and staying-power—especially in honouring their acting commitments—poor eyesight, bad memories, and intermittently indifferent health. They all possessed expressive hands—Fred's were beautiful (but Ellen's were not, though she used them wonderfully), and they all contrived to move with unfailing grace. Marion took the stage with immense distinction, even when bowed with age (there was a sensational moment one Christmas, when my mother warned us that Aunt Marion's hair was white and we must not appear to notice; she had always dyed it red which of course we had not realized), while Ellen appeared to dart across the scene, giving an impression of dragonfly swiftness and outdoor freedom. "But look where Beatrice, like a lapwing, runs close by the ground to hear our conference." Even when I saw her at the Coliseum and another time at a theatre on the West Pier at Brighton, during the First World War, acting the Trial Scene of *The Merchant of Venice* and some scenes as Mistress Page (with a young Edith Evans as Nerissa and Mistress Ford), she seemed to bring a breath of fresh air with her the moment she stepped on to the stage.

Ellen, Marion, and Fred—all three spoke with unerring diction, phrasing, and flow of thought, in the melting beauty of their inimitable Terry voices. As one can see from Ellen's rehearsal-scripts, she would rewrite and rephrase her lines as she tried to memorize them, in order to make them sound spontaneous and more natural, managing to breathe life into the stilted speeches allotted to her, even in fustian plays like *The Dead Heart* and *Ravenswood,* the later Irving productions at the Lyceum. Irving himself had always used the same method with his most famous parts (in his melodramas, *The Bells,* and *Louis XI,* for instance), and Fred used to follow the same example, cutting and adding continually over many performances to build up the effects he needed, though of course this was an impossible method to use in Shakespeare or in a really well-written modern play.

Fred could add grace to the most commonplace lines. As he leaned over the back of the garden seat in the scene at

Richmond in *The Scarlet Pimpernel* and said to Lady Blakeney "Madam, will you not dry those tears? I could never bear to see a pretty woman cry," he would suddenly lower his voice a whole octave and a hush would spread over the entire audience.

He loved to help young people if he possibly could, with money, encouragement, and good advice. He once sent for a young actor whom I knew and advised him to leave his company to take an engagement in the West End (this was towards the end of his own career, when he was touring with cheaper actors than before). He told the boy that he was ready to better himself and could learn no more from him. He helped to train the young Donald Wolfit, who always acknowledged all he had learned from him. When he was not acting himself he would go to see the current successes in the London theatres, standing at the back of the pit so that he could slip in and out unnoticed. He once engaged his nephew Gordon Craig to design a scene for him, though I doubt if he really understood his work. But he could never bring himself to appear in plays that he could not pretend to like and, in spite of recurring ill-health which he resisted with the greatest courage, he remained in management with his wife, acting in the vehicles they had always loved and in which they felt they both showed to the best advantage. They continued to give regular seasons in London with varying success, and managed to recover the losses of their occasional failures by touring the big provincial cities, where their arrivals and departures were always something of a royal progress.

Of course Fred should have played Falstaff in his later years, and he would have been a magnificent Sir Peter Teazle. But he preferred to act Benedick, for which he was then too old, and Bothwell and Henry the Eighth in two indifferent

melodramas, probably because they gave equal opportunities
to his wife. He had appeared as Charles Surface in his young
days, and told me that once, acting in the Screen Scene with
the famous old actor William Farren as Sir Peter, Mrs. Patrick
Campbell, hidden behind the screen as Lady Teazle, became exasperated by their slowness, and boomed out, "Oh,
do get on, you old pongers!" Someone congratulated him on
the way he flicked his lace handkerchief over his uncle's
portrait in the auction scene, but Fred only said modestly,
"Ah, that's Coghlan's business." It was always touching to
hear the respect and admiration he expressed for Irving and
his famous predecessors of the past.

When he first produced *The Scarlet Pimpernel* in the
provinces, it was not much liked, and Fred realized instinc-
tively that as nearly all the action took place offstage, a more
lively scene to open the play might get it off to a better
start. So a prologue was introduced, set at one of the Gates
of Paris, with the Pimpernel, disguised as an old woman,
driving a ramshackle cart in which, of course, the aristocrats
he was saving from The Terror were concealed. The new
opening proved an enormous success and the play was to
stand him in good stead for twenty years and more. As soon
as it became talked about, everyone got to know that the hag
in the Paris scene was Blakeney, despite his disguise of a
false nose and shabby bonnet, and the entrance of the cart
(drawn by a real horse—ever a hazardous but popular addi-
tion to any drama in those days) always drew a round of
applause to greet the star. But Fred soon decided that he need
not trouble to add to his labours by the task of making a
quick change of clothes and make-up so early in the evening,
and after a few weeks preferred to entrust the part of the old
hag to his obedient understudy. Of course the audience were

unaware of the deception and applauded just the same. But Fred instructed his dresser to stand in the wings at every performance and solemnly hand the Terry pince-nez to the understudy as he dismounted from the cart. It is not recorded whether the company were deceived by this charming little trick.

Fred's historical romances were always strictly wholesome, even at the expense of authenticity. Lady Castlemaine and the Duchess of Portsmouth were only malicious ladies at the court of the Merry Monarch, Nell Gwynne herself merely the King's great-hearted friend, who foiled the wicked Judge Jeffreys by dressing up in his wig and gown, making great comic play as she wielded a scratching quill pen and sneezed loudly after taking huge pinches of snuff. At the end of this scene she was triumphantly carried from the stage in a sedan-chair, waving her huge cartwheel feathered hat out of the window. She danced with two of her former actor cronies, accompanied herself on a spinet, and in the last act rushed breathlessly up a staircase from below in a magnificent dress which billowed round her, crying, "The Queen is too ill to see me. What's to be done?" The part of King Charles, with his real spaniels, was something of a holiday for Fred, but he wore a splendid make-up and played it to perfection, even when one of the dogs bit off the end of his false nose and jumped off his knee to vanish with it through the stage fireplace, to the audience's great delight.

He once mounted a production of *Romeo and Juliet* for his daughter Phyllis. He had intended to act Mercutio, but became ill during rehearsals and finally directed the play without appearing in it himself. A shy young actor, engaged to play the part of Paris, was given an elaborate Carpaccio costume to wear—parti-coloured tights and an Italianate wig falling to his shoulders. Some of the older members of the company, with whom he shared a dressing-room, mischievously drew attention to the inadequacy of his make-up, and finally persuaded him to add mascara to his eyelashes, rouge to his lips, and a dangling pearl to his right ear. Deeply self-conscious in all this finery, the young man slunk timidly on to the stage at the dress parade and bashfully announced himself. Fred, who was asleep in the darkness of the stalls, woke suddenly, rammed his glasses on to his nose, and, roaring with laughter, shouted out, "My God, it's a tart I once slept with in Bury St. Edmunds!"

At the old Borough Theatre, Stratford (long since torn down), on a foggy afternoon after a matinée, he came to the stage door, still dressed in his Pimpernel costume, to press a gold sovereign into my schoolboy hand. On another day he gave me a rich lunch at his Club, and afterwards climbed many flights of stairs in my parents' house to look at my model theatre and the clumsy scenery which I had painted to embellish it. Later, when his daughter had generously given me my first professional engagement, and afterwards, when I had arrived at some success, he never failed to encourage me and write me delightful letters. In one of them he praised my Hamlet, to my great delight, comparing it to that of Irving and Forbes-Robertson and the other great ones who had played the part. And though he professed to be deeply shocked by *The Constant Nymph* by Margaret Kennedy and Basil Dean (with its Gordon Craig-like character of the Bohemian Sanger, with his mistress and brood of illegitimate children) when he saw it in 1926, he seemed strangely tolerant of an equally ambiguous atmosphere when he came to see me act in Ronald MacKenzie's *Musical Chairs* in 1931. But by that year he had aged considerably, mellowing as his time grew short.

Narrow but generous, simple, direct, and deeply honest—a "prince of good fellows" (as he once called the Prince of Wales at a Public Dinner, only to find his Royal Highness furtively picking his nose as he sat beside him in the place of honour) he was a noble figure of the theatre, a consummate romantic actor, and a great gentleman besides.

3

BROTHER AND SISTER

EDWARD AND EDITH GORDON CRAIG

Edward and Edith Gordon Craig, the children of Ellen Terry by Edward Godwin, the architect and designer to whom she was never married, were a fascinating pair. The boy was something of a genius—a promising actor who became dissatisfied with acting, and became a brilliant designer, scene-inventor, etcher, woodcutter, and an accomplished and original writer; the girl, equally frustrated, was also an actress *manquée*, handsome, though less physically attractive, and gifted, like her brother, with considerable talents for which she failed, on the whole, to gain the recognition she deserved.

They were both devoted to their mother, but resented the absence of the father whom they had hardly known. Ellen's second husband, Charles Kelly, and afterwards Henry Irving, became substitute father-figures to them both, but they were difficult children to manage and were to cause their mother

continual anxiety as they grew older, even though her growing success and popularity, and the large salary which she
earned at the Lyceum, enabled her to lavish much care and
money on their education. She was inclined to spoil them,
though she tried to be very strict. Ted escaped from home
and married young, after a turbulent career at various schools
and a long restless apprenticeship at the Lyceum, but Edy
remained in her mother's house, failing to achieve an early
ambition to become a professional pianist through a rheu-
matic condition which developed when she was studying in
Germany.

Ellen Terry, remembering no doubt the failure of her own
marriages (the first, to the painter Watts, had been contracted
and dissolved when she was little more than a girl), is said to
have interfered on two occasions when Edy fell in love. A
clique of women friends who flattered and adored her gradually began to influence her strongly, and were apt to involve
her mother (whom they also adored) in jealous intrigues and
possessiveness. Ted never lived in England after his early
years, and, though Ellen loved him devotedly and treasured
his occasional visits, she had mostly to be content with pay-
ing his debts, sympathizing with the various women with
whom he was associated at different times, and housing his
children when he appeared to be too busy to look after them
himself.

The brother and sister were basically very fond of one another, but when they had worked together, under their
mother's management, at the Imperial Theatre in 1903, Ted
designing and directing and Edy in charge of the costume de-
partment, they had failed to get on for various reasons, and
Ted soon escaped abroad after the season had proved a disas-
trous financial failure. Though many had admired and praised
the ideas which he conceived in the few productions he had

actually carried out in London, he was obviously much before his time, and it was sad that no management had sufficient faith to engage him, as he was reputed to spend money extravagantly and demand to be given complete authority in any theatre in which he worked.

Ted and Edy had both appeared in minor parts with Irving and their mother at the Lyceum. Both became devoted to him, though the experience did not seem to give them great confidence in their own abilities as actors. Surprisingly for that strict time, they were accepted everywhere in society for Ellen Terry's sake, but there is no doubt that the slur of their illegitimacy, as well as a favouritism which they resented, helped to disturb their youthful development.

Edy was not aggressively masculine in personality, though she was sometimes brusque and rude, and very autocratic in dealing with those who worked with her. She was a very clever costume designer, and later an original stage director, but in her best years she was evidently too managing to be tactful or popular. Living in the shadow of Ellen Terry's overwhelming charm, she probably developed a complex about being considerably less attractive than her mother. She had a slight lisp which was hard for her to overcome, and she earned the reputation, as she grew older, of being a kind of dragon, apt to exploit her mother, bullying her, sometimes in front of other people, and forcing her to go on appearing in the theatre when her memory and eyesight were too weak to allow her to shine with her former lustre. Chris Marshall (who changed her name to Christopher St. John when she was converted to Catholicism) was Edy's greatest friend, and as devoted to the mother as she was to the daughter. She was the "literary henchman" who collaborated with Ellen in the writing of her splendid autobiography in 1906, the time of Ellen Terry's Jubilee. After Ellen died in 1928, she and Clare Atwood, the painter, helped Edy with devoted pains to perpetuate her memory, arranging Ellen's Smallhythe Farm as a beautiful museum, and adapting the old Barn which stands in her garden as a small theatre where they organized a matinée every year on the anniversary of her death. Christopher St. John also revised Ellen's first book of memoirs and annotated it admirably, while Edy, despite bitter recriminations from her brother (who retorted with a book *Ellen Terry and Her Secret Self* giving his own account of his relationship with his mother), persuaded Bernard Shaw to let her publish the fascinating correspondence between himself and Ellen Terry, which had originated when Shaw was a musical critic and Ellen was still leading lady at the Lyceum.

Edy was as industrious as her brother, and continued working almost till her death, producing plays in churches and pageants in parks and gardens. To me she was always most sympathetic and kindly, a picturesque figure whether in her country smock or rather striking Bohemian clothes, delivering her views with brisk authority. In old age she grew to look very like her mother. Many theatre people admired and respected her, though they were somewhat wary of allowing her too much rein for fear of upsetting her collaborators. She was unlucky to have lived at a time when women were not greatly trusted with leading positions in the world of the theatre (except as actresses) and in consequence she always had a good deal of suspicious resentment to contend with. Her mother became fretful and forgetful, and it was necessary for Edy to take every care of her. Her family resented this as an intrusion and criticized her accordingly, but there is no doubt that Ellen and Edy loved each other to the end, in spite of many difficulties and heart-burnings on both sides, fanned by the interference of well-meaning relations, as well as by enemies and devotees.

I appeared under Edy's direction for the first time at a matinée to help some Children's Charity at Daly's Theatre in the early Twenties. There were tableaux of famous Saints (Gladys Cooper as St. George, Sybil Thorndike as St. Joan) with groups of small children, dressed as cherubs and angels, in the main feature of the programme, a Nativity Play. The Virgin was to be played by Fay Compton, and I was asked to be one of the three shepherds. We had, I think, only one rehearsal, the usual half-baked muddle in some bleak room or other, with half the cast failing to put in an appearance. My own few lines were, I was told, to be spoken as the shepherds walked from the footlights across the stalls on a gangplank stretching to the back of the theatre. We had to sit down near the footlights, munch some food we had with us, and then see the Star in the East and move through the auditorium towards where it was supposed to be.

On the afternoon of the performance the house was not very full. In fact there seemed to be more people on the stage and behind the scenes than in the audience. The mothers of the children who were appearing kept rushing from their seats in the stalls, pushing through the pass door in to the wings to attend to their offspring's manifold emergencies. Stage-hands were trying to find their way among the crowd of actors and actresses who were greeting one another in loud stage whispers. Two huge wolfhounds were held on leashes by Esmé Percy, who was Herod, and George Hayes, his decadent son. Edith Craig herself, with her devoted friends, Christopher St. John and Clare Atwood, dressed in voluminous monks' robes, were issuing orders in all directions. As the afternoon wore on and a number of mistakes began to occur, they drew their hoods over their heads and pressed their way on to the stage among the performers. I entered with my two companions, and we proceeded towards the footlights, where we sat to begin our speeches, to find, to our dismay, that slices of delicious soft bread, hunks of cheese, and apples had been realistically provided in our haversacks. These, rashly crammed into our mouths, made our enunciation almost unintelligible. However we hastily finished our lines (and our food) and progressed gingerly towards the doors at the back of the stalls, only to find them locked impenetrably against our exit. So we had to walk back along the ramp the way we had come, and sneak as unobtrusively as we could round the characters on the stage who were already engaged in playing another scene.

After the episode in which Joseph and Mary arrived at the inn and were given shelter in the stable, there was supposed to be a blackout, during which the Child was born, to be discovered later in the manger with the Virgin and the animals. But the light cues were fatally mismanaged, and the gauze, supposed to conceal the stable during an interlude played in front of it, suddenly became transparent. Fay Compton could be plainly seen picking up the doll representing the infant Jesus by its heels out of the crib and swathing it with a napkin before setting it on her lap. Ellen Terry, who had been brought by her daughter to make an appeal at the beginning of the performance, and was now sitting in the prompt corner, eagerly listening to all that was going on, peered through her thick spectacles at Fay Compton and called out in her famous Terry whisper, "Do tell that child to take all that red off her lips."

Ted Craig was a great disappointment to me when I met him first. C. B. Cochran had invited him to England to design an opening production for the Phoenix Theatre, which had just been completed in 1930. Sidney Bernstein had built it and had engaged Komisarjevsky to decorate it. Sidney lent Craig his London house to stay in and he was given *carte*

Jane Cowl

While she was in England, Miss Cowl wrote a play with the English
actress Joyce Carey (daughter of Lilian Braithwaite) entitled
Hervey House. It was presented at His Majesty's Theater in 1935
starring Fay Compton and Gertrude Lawrence. (I was nearly in the play
myself in the role eventually played by Nicholas Hannen.) Margaret
Rutherford made one of her first successes in a supporting part, as did
Alan Webb, but the play only achieved a brief engagement even
though directed by Tyrone Guthrie. During the weeks they were
awaiting rehearsals, the two authors made a tour of Devonshire riding
bicycles, while a Rolls-Royce followed them distantly in case they
became tired.

John Barrymore as Hamlet at the Theatre Royal, Haymarket, 1925

Playing Hamlet at the Haymarket Theatre in London in 1925, Barrymore was considered a somewhat alarming partner by the English company, greatly as they admired his performance.

More than one Laertes was savagely injured in the last act, and had to be hastily replaced while Fay Compton, his enchanting Ophelia, found herself flung down on the floor one evening during the Nunnery Scene. When she reproved him later for his violent behavior, he answered, "I couldn't resist it when I saw those tears running down your cheeks, like rain on little russet apples."

After a Memorial Service in London to commemorate a delightful and popular actor, I happened to meet Lilian Braithwaite and we walked up the street to lunch together.

The actor's widow, once a moderately successful actress, had retired from the stage some years before her husband's death. On several occasions she had loyally extricated him from one or two amorous entanglements, and now we watched her as she left the service, on the arm of her elder son, at the head of the congregation. Lilian did not speak for a few moments as we strolled away. Then I heard her murmer in her rather dreamy voice, "Poor old Mary! That's what comes of putting all your eggs in one basket."

Lilian Braithwaite

Vivien Leigh

blanche by Cochran to decide on the play he would choose to design and perhaps also to direct. I was acting at the Old Vic at the time, my second season there, and *The Tempest,* in which I was playing Prospero, had just been added to the repertoire. Of course I was greatly excited at the prospect of meeting my famous second cousin. As a schoolboy I had devoured his books, the more enthusiastically since Ellen Terry herself had given me one of them, *On the Art of the Theatre,* as a Christmas present with a dedication written on the title page. Craig invited me to lunch at the Café Royal. With him was Martin Shaw, a clever musician and one of Craig's oldest and dearest friends. They had produced *Dido and Aeneas* and *Acis and Galatea* together in Hampstead at the beginning of the century. Martin Shaw was disfigured by a large birthmark on one side of his face, and, according to one account, Edy had once been in love with him, but Ellen had considered him too ill-looking for her daughter.

Craig treated me somewhat patronizingly at this first meeting. He said, "I felt we ought to get to know each other, as you seem to be quite popular here in London." He went on to say that he had rushed from the Old Vic in horror after seeing only the opening scene of *The Tempest,* though Harcourt Williams, who had directed the production, was one of his old friends and fellow actors. Ted had written to him several times during our rehearsals, wishing him luck and predicting success for him, and Harcourt Williams had continually held him up to us all as a great man and an acknowledged genius of the theatre, so I was naturally very hurt by his airy dismissal of Lilian Baylis, the Vic, and all it stood for. Naturally, too, my vanity was piqued that he had seen so little of my own performance. I asked him shyly what play he was proposing to do for Cochran. "Oh," he answered vaguely, "I am not sure yet. Perhaps *Macbeth.* I have many schemes and designs for that play. But, you know, what I do look forward to is inviting any artists or friends who may be in London at the time to sit with me in the Royal Box and watch rehearsals." I took this remark with a grain of salt, but throughout our meal I felt that he was probably posing a good deal and pulling my leg. Still, I went away with a great sense of disappointment. Not long afterwards the whole project with Cochran ended in smoke and Craig went back to Italy, and it was many years—twenty-two to be exact—before I was to see him again.

In 1953 I had rented a villa in the South of France for a summer holiday, and decided to look him up in Vence, where he was living on little money at a small pension. My sister and I drove up a steep lane to find it, and there, standing at the top of a flight of stone steps, was Craig—unmistakably impressive in a broad-brimmed straw hat, with a walking stick (probably Irving's) in his hand, large tortoise-shell spectacles on his nose, a scarf thrown round his neck, and a frieze Italian cloak flung back over a white coat like a surgeon's, with a high collar, and some kind of medallion on a black cord round his neck. He looked very like the famous Toulouse-Lautrec poster of Aristide Bruant. He seemed enormously pleased to welcome us, sang snatches of music-hall songs, cracked jokes, and told us the best restaurant to eat at. Of coure we took him there immediately and helped him to enjoy a delicious meal. Then he took us back to the pension and showed us his small room, touchingly simple and beautifully arranged. Small photographs were pinned on a screen and above his narrow little bed with its folded rug. Pipes, drawing instruments, knives and chisels, all impeccably tidy, were laid out in order on his desk. He had created a little world of his own in those modest surroundings. On a shelf were copies of mid-Victorian farces which he had collected on the quais in Paris and bound and annotated himself. Books were piled everywhere but he seemed to know exactly where to find any reference he wanted. He seemed contented and delightfully affable, and when he came to see us at our villa a few days later he charmed us as greatly as before. I noticed that he never spoke French—even in the restaurant, where the proprietress and waiters knew him well—and he seemed amazingly well informed about the theatre in London and indeed everywhere in Europe. He had met Laurence Olivier in Paris, where he had seen him play Richard the Third, and thought his performance fine and Irvingesque. I told him I had heard he had gone to see it several times. "Yes," he replied, "I am getting deaf you know, and they used to let me pop into the prompter's box so that I could see and hear really well." "Surely not *every* night," I said. "Well, occasionally I used to slip out and sit for a bit of a smoke in the box-office," he admitted, chuckling. "And do you know, about nine o'clock every evening a man would come in and take a big bag of money away with him. Of course that impressed me very much!"

We had broken the ice at last on these two visits, and I was deeply touched when, at a time of great trouble for me in London a few months later, he suddenly wrote me a letter enclosing a card in Ellen Terry's handwriting, which she had sent to comfort him on some occasion, years before, when he had been involved in a disturbing crisis of his own.

After that time we wrote to each other fairly often, and I went to see him again whenever I was in the South of France. After long negotiations he had managed to sell his fine library to a French collector, and with the money had bought a small bungalow on the outskirts of Vence, where he was looked after by his daughter Nellie, a charming middle-aged woman, about my sister's age, with a great look of her grandmother and a gentle voice. He was ninety now, deaf, toothless,

and very frail, but still full of energy and fun. He was lying
on his bed when we arrived to take him out to lunch, reading
a little book of Elizabethan poems. I asked Nellie to come
with us (at which she seemed rather surprised, as she had expected to be left at home) and we got into the car with Ted
in front. He chose a restaurant some fifteen miles away and
seemed delighted at the prospect of quite a long drive. "Don't
talk at the back there," he shouted to us, "I can't hear a word
you're saying." Then he handed the book of poems to me
across the back of his seat. "Read this one," he said, "it's supposed to be by Walter Raleigh, but it's far too good for that.
I bet it's Shakespeare. You ought to read it in your Recital,
John, I hear you're having a great success with your readings."
"All right," I said, "if you'll copy it out in your beautiful
handwriting and send it to me." But, alas he never did.

We chattered and laughed together over an enormous
lunch, and it was after four o'clock when we got back to his
little villa. When I said goodbye he put his hands on my
shoulders and kissed me sweetly on both cheeks, and I felt
sure I would not see him again.

Was Craig a genius? Thinking of him the other day I suddenly wondered why on earth I did not ask him to design
Macbeth for me when I directed and played in it in 1942—
but then of course the war was raging, and he could not easily
have come to England. (He was actually interned in Paris by
the Nazis, but released after a few months with the help of
Sylvia Beach, the publisher, and some Germans who had always admired his work.) But I fancy he would always have
proved very difficult to handle if he had ever got down to the
concrete task of producing a play. He was didactic and un-
compromising, but also frivolous and unpredictable, as one
can easily see from his son Edward's superb biography. Apart
from the management who engaged him would he have

known how to deal with actors and actresses? Would he have been patient and tactful enough to direct them, as he always seemed to expect to be allowed to do, as well as collaborating successfully with the technicians in creating the décor and lighting? He suffered from persecution mania, relying on other people yet trusting hardly anyone. He could not bring himself to confide in those who tried or offered to carry out his ideas for fear they would steal or misinterpret them. Autocratic to a degree, wildly egotistical, fickle and utterly unprincipled where money and women were concerned, he still created for himself a mystique of enduring proportions.

A master without a school, an Englishman hardly acknowledged in his own country, he influenced the whole development of the theatre both in Europe and America. He abolished footlights and experimented with the spatial limits of the stage both in his designs and in one or two of the few productions which he actually achieved, framing his scenes in higher and wider proscenium openings and creating effects of simplicity and grandeur. He used a cyclorama for the first time, and the movable screens which he designed for the Moscow Art's production of *Hamlet* by Stanislavsky (though they failed to be completely successful on that occasion through lack of technical equipment to manipulate them), were a really magnificent invention. His passion for research was indefatigable. He was a voracious reader and an untiring worker. Very beautiful as a young man, his features still had a certain weakness which remained even when he was very old. Temperamental, crackety, with a charming voice and aristocratic manner, he was an artist to his fingertips. His thumbs however were rather sinister—unnaturally broad and thick. Quarrelsome and tender, violent one minute and gentle the next, he must always have been what nurses used to call "a handful!"

4

THREE WITTY LADIES

MRS. PATRICK CAMPBELL, LADY TREE, AND DAME LILIAN BRAITHWAITE

MRS. PATRICK CAMPBELL

"Stella—Stella for Star," cried the heroine of Tennessee Williams's *Streetcar Named Desire*. And I thought at once of another star—Stella Beatrice, the great actress Mrs. Patrick Campbell. Brilliant, impossible, cruel, fascinatingly self-destructive, witty (especially when she had a foeman worthy of her steel—Herbert Tree, Bernard Shaw, or Noël Coward), devastatingly unpredictable, she could be grandly snobbish one minute and generously simple the next. She despised people who were afraid of her, would patronize an audience if she felt them to be unsympathetic, and make fun of her fellow actors if they failed to provide her with inspiration. I once saw her walk through the whole of the first act of Ibsen's *John Gabriel Borkman,* ignoring the other players and taking every other line from the prompter, only to electrify the house in the next scene when she was partnered by an actor she admired. Her stage movements were expressive and unlike those of any other actress. I can see her now in *The Second Mrs. Tanqueray* by Sir Arthur Wing Pinero (late in her career, on tour at a theatre in Croydon), peeling muscat grapes with her fingers and cramming them into her mouth, "I adore fruit, especially when it's expensive"; stabbing the hat on her lap with a furious hatpin as Mrs. Cortelyon left the stage in the second act, and gazing at her face in a hand-mirror at the end of the play just before her final exit. I see her opening champagne in *Ghosts,* laying a table, cooing to a baby, and digging into a hamper of old clothes in *The Matriarch,* a play based on the novel by G. B. Stern, knitting in the last act of *Pygmalion* with a look of unutterable boredom on her face, airing her newly taught society accent in hollow, supercilious tones.

She was beginning to be fat when I met her first, and would make constant references to her fast-vanishing figure. "I look like a burst paper bag," and, "I must borrow a chair with a high back so that I can hide my chins behind it." She nearly always wore sweeping black dresses and hats with shady brims (she once told me proudly that the hat she was wearing that day looked so much better since she had trimmed the edges of it with a pair of nail-scissors), and her flowing velvets were usually sprinkled with the white hairs of Moonbeam, her beloved Pekinese. But she still appeared majestic as she swept down in the hotel lift to enthrone herself in a New York taxi, where she would proceed to chat with the driver on a variety of topics—the stupidity of Hollywood, the Abdication of the Duke of Windsor ("Such a gesture has not been made since Antony gave up a Kingdom for Cleopatra") or the necessity of a halt to walk her dog. "Who's responsible for this?" the man demanded as he discovered a puddle on the floor of his cab. "I am," replied Mrs. Campbell, as she alighted calmly.

Everyone referred to her as Mrs. Pat, but I always hated the familiarity, and took care always to address her by her full name until the day when she rewarded me by asking me to call her Stella. I had been introduced to her, in the early Twenties, at a luncheon party in Brighton in a private suite at the Metropole Hotel given by a Lord who loved the stage. She was playing Hedda Gabler at a theatre on one of the piers (why didn't I go to see her in it?) and someone told her that the performance was a *tour de force*. "I suppose that is why I am always forced to tour," she replied mournfully. Her company dreaded her, except for the few worshippers who dared to stand up to her when she was in a bad mood. She loved rich and titled people and would allow them to give her presents and entertain her, but she was very proud with younger folk and generous both in advice and criticism. She could be wonderful company, though I think she was often cruel to men who fell in love with her—even Forbes-Robertson and Shaw—and sometimes even more unkind to her women friends, letting them fetch and carry for her for a time and then making fun of them or casting them aside. But somehow I was never afraid of her, though the only time I acted with her, as Oswald in *Ghosts* in 1929, she played some alarming tricks and made a fool of me at one performance. The dress-rehearsal had gone off without mishap, and Mrs. Campbell was word perfect and sailing through her scenes. At the first performance, however, she seemed less at ease, though still charming to me at the fall of the curtain, when she graciously thanked me for having helped her through. I beamed with delight and thought I had passed my test. At the second performance I was sitting at a table smoking. No ash tray had been provided, and I looked helplessly round when the cue came for me to put out my cigar. Not daring to leave my chair, for fear of complicating the moves that had been arranged by the director, I stubbed it out on the chenille tablecloth and dropped the butt under the table and then, a few moments later, stupidly put my hands on the table before lifting them to cover my face. Mrs. Campbell, turning upstage, shook with laughter for the rest of the scene, and pouted, "Oh, you're such an amateur!" as the curtain fell. During the second interval my aunt, Mabel Terry-Lewis, never famous for her tact, burst into my dressing-room. "Tell her we can't hear a word she says," she announced, "the Charing Cross Road is being drilled outside!" This counsel I naturally preferred to ignore, though it hardly tended to improve my already shaken confidence. But worse was yet to come. At the end of the play Mrs. Alving stands aghast, staring at her son as he mutters, "Mother, give me the sun. The sun! The sun!" In her hand she still holds the box of pills which she does not dare to give him. Mrs. Campbell had evidently decided suddenly that she must make the most of this important final moment. With a wild cry, she flung the pillbox into the footlights and threw herself across my knees with her entire weight. "Oswald. Oswald!" she moaned. The armchair (borrowed by Mrs. Campbell herself from a friend, because, as she said, "the back is high enough to hide my chins") cracked ominously as she lay prone across my lap, and as I clutched the arms in desperation for fear they might disintegrate, she whispered fiercely, "Keep down for the call. This play is worse than having a confinement." Yet she had been of the greatest help during rehearsals and I always thought she could, if she had chosen, have been a fine director herself.

It was very difficult to judge the extent of her real talents in those later days. Of course I never saw her at the time of her early triumphs, when she was slim and elegant and Aubrey Beardsley drew her, willow-slender, for an exquisite study in black-and-white. I think she never took much exercise— the leading ladies of her day didn't deign to walk—and she was very fond of food. During the rehearsals of *Ghosts* we would lunch together, and she would sit in the Escargot Restaurant, devouring snails by the dozen. One day, while we were there, a striking-looking lady, with black hair parted in the middle and drawn back in a great knot at the nape of her neck, appeared in the doorway, attracting considerable attention from everyone in the room. "Surely that is Madame Marguerite D'Alvarez, the famous singer," I ventured to remark. Mrs. Campbell lifted her eyes from her plate and murmured in tragic tones, "Ah yes, Me in a spoon."

I thought she did not much care for the Terry family, for my great-aunt Marion had been a famous rival of hers. She had played Mrs. Erlynne on one occasion in Dublin to Mrs. Campbell's Lady Windermere, and taken over her part at the last moment when Mrs. Campbell quarrelled with Forbes-Robertson during the rehearsals of Henry Arthur Jones' *Michael and His Lost Angel,* though Marion proved to be ill-suited and the play was a complete failure. They were to play together once more in the 1920 revival of *Pygmalion,* and I fancy that she and Mrs. Campbell must have worked on this occasion with velvet gloves. But she always spoke to me of Ellen Terry with great admiration though she could not resist one crushing remark about my mother's family. I had been distressed to find her in New York (this was in 1936), living without a maid in a second-rate hotel room, clothes and papers strewn everywhere, laid up with influenza. She wrote afterwards to Shaw that my eyes had filled with tears when I arrived. "All the Terrys cry so easily," was her typical comment. But when I tried to send her a cheque as a Christmas present she refused to accept it and sent it back.

One afternoon, while I was playing *Hamlet* in New York, Mrs. Campbell offered to take me to visit Edward Sheldon, the playwright. This remarkable man had been a youthful friend of John Barrymore, and had encouraged him to further his stage career by the brilliant series of classical revivals and romantic plays (*Richard III, Hamlet,* Tolstoy's *Living Corpse, The Jest*) in which Barrymore triumphed in the early Twenties. Sheldon was also the author of two sensationally successful melodramas, *Salvation Nell* for Mrs. Fiske and *Romance* for Doris Keane, with whom he had been very much in love. He was now completely paralyzed and blind as a result of some petrifying bone disease, but, despite his infirmity, he retained all his intellectual faculties, and continued his friendship with all the most brilliant players of the New York theatre, who went continually to see him and greatly valued his advice.

I realized, of course, that it was a great compliment to be given the opportunity of this meeting, and arrived punctually at the address in the East Sixties where he lived. Mrs. Campbell was not yet there, and I was somewhat dismayed to be shown up to the penthouse, where I was ushered in to a big lofty room with many windows looking out on to a terrace. Flowers, photographs, and books were everywhere, and there was no feeling of a sickroom except for the great bed, covered with a dark brocade coverlet, on which Sheldon lay stretched out, with his head tilted back at what seemed a dreadfully low and uncomfortable angle. His smooth face was beautifully shaved and he wore a neat bow tie and a soft shirt, but his eyes were covered with a black mask, and his hands were invisible beneath the coverlet.

Of course I was very shy at first, but as soon as he began to talk (though with a grating tired voice) he managed immediately to put me at my ease, and by the time Mrs. Campbell arrived we were chattering away as if we had known each other all our lives.

Books and newspapers were read to him every day, and he

was amazingly well-informed, especially about the theatre, and seemed to know everything that was going on. He asked me if I would come again one day and act some scenes from *Hamlet* for him, and of course I promised to do so. Again, he contrived to put me at my ease, and I never played to a more sensitive and appreciative audience.

In the years that followed he never forgot me, sending cables and messages even during the war years (he was destined to live longer than Mrs. Campbell, who died in 1940) and when I was acting in Congreve's *Love for Love* in 1944 I received a telegram, HOW I WISH I COULD SEE YOU IN VALENTINE'S MAD SCENE.*

On that first afternoon, Mrs. Campbell appeared ten minutes after I did. I fancy Sheldon had asked her to be late, so that he could break the ice with me alone. She was in one of her complaining moods, pouting and holding up her Pekinese against Sheldon's face, sighing that nobody wanted her any more in the theatre now that she was old and fat. Sheldon suddenly grew very quiet, and I noted how quickly she changed her manner and began to behave and talk in the fascinating, brilliant way that showed her at her very best. When we went away I tried to tell her how much I appreciated her charming gesture in taking me to see Sheldon and how delightfully she had helped to entertain us both. "Ah," she said, with real sincerity, "one has to be at one's best with Ned. After all, we are all he has left. Think of it. There he lies in that room up there which he will never leave, and here we are walking in the street in the sunshine." I never loved her more than on that day.

---

* The remarkable memories of the older well-educated generation are very striking. Mr Justice Frankfurter, the noted U. S. Supreme Court Justice, quoted verbatim the whole opening scene of *Love for Love* when I met him in Washington at supper after the performance.

In a lecture recital which she concocted in the early Thirties, I realized that she was a complete Pre-Raphaelite. Neither Shakespeare nor the Bible served to exhibit her to real advantage. She boomed too much, sometimes even verging upon absurdity. I once saw her attempt Lady Macbeth, appearing with the American actor James Hackett, and she evidently did not care for acting with him. She had one fine moment at the end of the banquet scene, when she wearily dragged the crown from her head and her black hair fell to her shoulders as she sat huddled on the throne. But on her first appearance, looking like the Queen of Hearts about to have the gardeners executed, she swept her eyes over the stalls, graciously bowed to acknowledge her reception—leading ladies always entered to applause in those days—and, solemnly unrolling a large scroll (which, as one critic remarked, it would have taken a whole monastery a month to illuminate!), she read out Macbeth's letter with stately emphasis but ill-concealed contempt. In her recital, however, the excerpts from Pinero, Shaw, and Ibsen were very fine, and I was especially impressed by her rendering of *The High Tide on the Lincolnshire Coast,* a Victorian poem by Jean Ingelow. Her success with this made me realize why she had been so greatly in demand at parties in the Nineties, when she would recite (no doubt for an enormous fee) "Butterflies all White— Butterflies all Black," in competition with Sarah Bernhardt, who was also a fashionable diseuse at the smart houses in those days whenever she acted in London. The two stars became great cronies, and on one occasion they played *Pelléas and Mélisande* together in French. Mrs. Campbell had played Mélisande before with Martin Harvey and Forbes-Robertson, and in her recital she used to give an excerpt from that play (in English naturally), delivering the speeches of both the lovers in two contrasting voices, but this was not a very happy experiment as it seemed to me. The two actresses were fond of exchanging long telegrams with one another. I think Stella was not, as Ellen Terry was, an inspired letter-writer, and her correspondence with Shaw compares very poorly with that of Ellen. But I well remember a small luncheon party which I gave in New York when Mrs. Campbell read to us aloud an article she had written on Bernhardt for a theatre magazine. This was charmingly written and immensely moving, and, of course, drew more "Terry tears" from me.

She had always been amused to shock people by her behaviour, though she was sometimes rather prudish too, and I took care never to make ambiguous jokes when I was with her. My mother told me that once at a dinner party, when Stella was first married, she made a sensation, as the ladies rose to leave the table, by seizing a handful of cigars as they were being passed to the gentlemen by a servant, and, sticking them boldly in her *décolletage* one by one, announced gaily, "Poor Pat can't afford cigars."

Her witticisms have become a legend. Of Noël Coward's dialogue, "His characters talk like typewriting." Of a leading lady she was acting with, "Her eyes are so far apart that you want to take a taxi from one to the other." "Tell Mr. Alexander [who was playing Tanqueray] I never laugh at him while we are on the stage together. I always wait till I get home." Of Shaw, "One day he will eat a beefsteak, and then God help us poor women." But Alexander Woollcott's famous remark after her Hollywood film débâcle a few years before she died, "She is like a sinking ship firing on its rescuers," was sadly to the point. She became impossibly difficult, insulted managers who made her offers, appeared in one or two absurdly bad plays, and made them worse by clowning in the serious scenes and assuming a tragic manner in the light ones. When she was appearing in a light comedy of Ivor Novello's in New York, for instance, she insisted on interpolating a speech from *Electra* in the middle of a most unsuitable context. But she never lost her sense of style or her regal bearing, and the deep voice, so often imitated, retained its thrilling range and power. James Agate still talked of "the questing sweep of her throat" and her feet and ankles were slim and elegant to the last.

I read one of the lessons at her Memorial Service in 1941, on the morning following a first night at the Old Vic at which I had essayed King Lear. Coming out of the church I heard someone say, "It was an exciting occasion at the Old Vic last night," and the answer, "Yes, until the curtain went up," was, I felt, one that Stella's shade would have surely relished. She might so easily have delivered it herself.

LADY TREE

Lady Tree, *née* Maud Holt, had been a medical student and a Greek scholar before she became a successful actress. In her early photographs she appears pretty and slight, but when I first saw her on the stage, and later when I came to meet her, she had become somewhat eccentric-looking, wearing strikingly coloured flowing robes and fantastic hats, with scarves and veils draped about her throat and shoulders. She was supposed to have been a most moving Ophelia, when her husband, Sir Herbert Beerbohm Tree, played Hamlet. In his fair wig and beard Max Beerbohm is said to have remarked that he looked like a German Professor, and described his performance as being "funny without being vulgar," though Max was always too much of a gentleman to attack his half-brother in his official notices in the *Saturday Review*.

Invited to see a play one evening by some enthusiastic

friends, Max was somewhat dismayed to be ushered into a box at His Majesty's to see a performance of *Hamlet*. During the evening his hosts looked round to find his chair unoccupied, but soon found him curled up on a pile of overcoats in the passage, dozing. He woke and murmured apologetically, "I am so sorry. I always enjoy Herbert's Hamlet this way."

Sir Herbert was brilliant and eccentric too. He emulated a number of his contemporaries in siring several offspring besides those already presented him by his wife. Lady Tree, playing hostess, was once heard to remark, "Ah, Herbert, late again? Another confinement in Putney?" And one night, returning late from a party to find Sir Herbert supping *tête à tête* with Esmé Percy, an extremely handsome young actor in his company, she peeped in at the door and murmured, "The port's on the sideboard, Herbert, and remember it's adultery just the same."

Many years later she was acting in *The Mask of Virtue,* a comedy in an eighteenth-century setting adapted from the French, in which Vivien Leigh made her first success in London. At the dress rehearsal Lady Tree, gazing hopefully across the empty stalls, called to the director, "Mr. A., it seems a little dark on the stage in this scene. Could you oblige us with a little more light? I think you may not have realized that my comedic effects in this play are almost wholly grimacial."

At a charity matinée in which I once appeared with her she surveyed her script at rehearsals through an enormous magnifying glass. I was told that she would bring *The Times* Crossword Puzzle into the wings with her and proceed to solve it during her waits, uttering strange syllabic gasps and grunts to find the word of the exact length and shape she needed. Once in a modern comedy, *Indoor Fireworks,* she seemed to have threaded a lace scarf from one side of her head to the other, passing it through her large red wig and finally tying it

under her chin like a bonnet, achieving a very strange result.
One day I was lunching in a Soho restaurant, before playing a
matinée, and saw her arrive at a neighbouring table with her
daughter Viola. Not expecting her to remember me I bowed
respectfully in passing them as I rose to go. Halfway down
the street I heard my name called after me in dulcet tones,
and, looking back, saw Lady Tree standing in the doorway of
the restaurant, waving her scarf to me in belated greeting like
Isolde or some Arthurian heroine of romance.

When she lay dying in hospital, her lawyer came to see her
to help her to put her affairs in order. When he had gone
away, her daughter asked her if his visit had not too greatly
tired her. "Not at all," said Lady Tree. "He was just teaching
me my death duties."

DAME LILIAN BRAITHWAITE

I knew Dame Lilian Braithwaite very well, and also had the
delight of working with her very often. Since her early days
as a successful *ingénue,* she had acted in every kind of play—
farce, melodrama, Shakespeare—and was already a well-
known leading lady in a number of West End plays at the
time of the First World War. She was considered at that time
to be a somewhat sentimental actress of sympathetic parts.
But when she made an astonishing success as the vapid man-
hunting society mother in Noël Coward's *The Vortex* in
1924, critics and public were full of praise for her courage in
daring to play with such honesty and conviction. From this
new success she continued from one triumph to another both
in light comedies and dramatic plays. Her witty timing, which
she used to perfection both on and off the stage, gave a delicious edge to what seemed at first a deceptively innocent air
of conventional Edwardian charm. Her kindness was unfail-

ing, but the subtlety of the pause she would give to cap a critical remark could be delightfully pungent and occasionally devastating. "B. told me that she is off to do a play in New York tomorrow . . . but I don't think it can be a very big part as she is going on a very small boat." "Of course I'm very fond of G. . . . , but I know what people mean." I was with her once at a matinée. One of the leading actresses appearing in the play was known to be distinctly plain, but in a romantic-looking photograph displayed in the programme she appeared as a raving beauty. Lilian glanced at the picture, murmured, "Fancy!" and quickly turned the page. She was a beautiful woman, always looking cool and elegant both on and off the stage, and she managed her cooing voice and precise diction with impeccable skill. She could drawl in an affected part or dominate in a dramatic scene with unexpected power. I used to watch her, fascinated, as she waited to make her first entrance in *The Vortex,* standing behind the closed door at which she was to appear, bracing herself with deep breaths, like an athlete preparing for a race, before she opened it.

She was a worthy opponent for some of her witty contemporaries, and could even challenge Mrs. Campbell and Marie Tempest on their own ground, if either of them tried to patronize her, as they sometimes did. Lunching at the Ivy Restaurant one day with her daughter, a very unattractive man appeared in the doorway. The *maître d'hôtel* enquired politely, "You want a table, sir? For two?" "No," replied the man, "I'm quite alone." Lilian was heard to mutter, "I'm not surprised."

Her enthusiasm and gallantry never failed her. In the Second War she went on organizing concerts and entertainments for ENSA* as well as appearing herself with unfailing pro-

* Entertainments National Service Association.

fessionalism and punctuality in the theatre in several long and arduous runs. Returning late one night after acting in *Arsenic and Old Lace,* she took refuge in the ground floor cloakroom during a big air raid lasting for many hours. Asked the next morning if she was not exhausted by the experience she replied smilingly, "Certainly not. We were fifty pounds up last night." To a young actress who rashly remarked, "Oh, I am so sorry you were in front this afternoon. I always feel I must save myself for the evening performance," Lilian only shook her head, "I didn't think you saved anything," she said. And at a magnificent party to celebrate a long run she pointed to her dress with the remark "C. has given me a dear little diamond brooch . . . can you see it?"

Actresses seemed in my youth to achieve astonishing changes in their figures in order to suit the fashions of the time. Lilian Braithwaite, a wasp-waisted slim *ingénue* in her early photographs, looked almost ample when I first saw her, during the First War, as the heroine's mother in a play at the Haymarket, *General Post,* with Norman McKinnel, Madge Titheradge, and George Tully. But ten years later she was as slim as a reed in the tubular frocks, short skirts, and shingled hair of the dancing mother in *The Vortex.* Even Ellen Terry, graceful and elegant until the end of the last century, appears matronly and almost stout in the photographs of her in *Captain Brassbound's Conversion* in 1906, though she too became extremely slender in her old age. Yet these were the days before dieting and beauty parlours. Marie Tempest was always plump and Yvonne Arnaud increasingly so as time went on. Lilian could not resist saying of her, "It's still the dear little face we all loved so in *By Candle Light* [Pause]—but there's another face round it."

The three actresses in this chapter might have perhaps been ideally cast as the three Queens in *Alice in Wonderland*

—their dialogue precisely to the point, their wit as characteristically individual as their delightful and original personalities. Their witticisms would certainly have provided remarkable copy for anyone lucky enough to overhear what they had to say to one another behind the scenes.

During the Boer War, Lady Tree would appear at music halls, appealing for charity, and was fond of reciting Kipling's poem "The Absent-Minded Beggar." She would enter, magnificently dressed, and, after acknowledging the applause that greeted her appearance, would raise her hand and announce confidingly to the audience, "Now I want you all to picture me as a very old cab-driver."

Lady Tree, 1935

On the wall of a house in Pont Sreet, Knightsbridge, in London, the London County Council have affixed a blue plaque recording that the house was for many years the home of Sir George Alexander. When I first met Mrs. Campbell, some years after Alexander's death, she was living in an apartment in Pont Street just opposite this very house, and I sometimes used to go to visit her there. A few years ago a similar plaque was put up on a house in Kensington Square, where Mrs. Campbell had lived years earlier when she was enjoying many of her greatest successes in London. No doubt the LCC were tactful enough to resist honouring her memory in Pont Street, where her plaque would have faced that of the actor-manager with whom she had waged so many battles in the past.

Mrs. Patrick Campbell, 1913

The system of "blackballs" (in anonymous disapproval) has long been a tradition of the great clubs of London.

A noted but somewhat unpopular director applied for admission to the famous Garrick Club, and, when he failed to obtain sufficient nominations, the Committee requested Sir Gerald, as the most tactful of distinguished actors, to undertake to break the news to the unlucky applicant. Du Maurier invited the director to take sherry with him in a private room at the club, and tried to indicate somewhat apologetically that his application had been refused. The director turned very white and enquired, "Were there many dissensions?" Whereupon, Du Maurier, embarrassed by the whole affair, lost his head and blurted out, "Ever heard of sheep shit?"

Gerald du Maurier in *Interference* at St. James's Theatre, 1927

The story of Hawtrey and Brookfield celebrating Oscar Wilde's condemnation by giving a supper party has been recently denied categorically by Rupert Croft-Cooke in an interesting biography in which he examines the truth and falsehood of the various books and legends about Wilde which have accumulated over the last seventy years. As a great admirer of Hawtrey, I never liked to believe the story myself, though it was told me in my youth by several people whose veracity I trusted. Charles Brookfield acted the part of Lord Goring's (Hawtrey) valet in the original production of *An Ideal Husband* and was said to have only accepted it because it was the smallest part in the play. He is certainly known to have disliked Wilde, who once called a rehearsal on Christmas Eve which was very unpopular with the company. "Don't you keep Christmas, Oscar?" Brookfield remarked and Wilde retorted with some smart reply. Brookfield was a good actor, was himself the author of several plays, and later became Censor of plays in London.

Charles Hawtrey in *Ambrose Applejohn's Adventure* at the Criterion Theatre, 1921

The Circle at the Theatre Royal, Haymarket, 1921. Round the table left to right, Toni Edgar Bruce, Lottie Venne, Leon Quartermaine, and Allan Aynesworth with E. Holman Clark (standing)

The Circle was a failure on its opening night in London, just after the First World War. Lottie Venne was nervous and the gallery shouted to her to speak up. When I saw the production some weeks later, I found her performance inimitable, but the play was before its time and shocked the prim Haymarket Theatre audience by its cynicism. The part of Lady Kitty was afterwards taken in two revivals first by Athene Seyler and then by Yvonne Arnaud, (the latter under my own management in 1944), but neither of these two fine actresses played it as perfectly as Lottie Venne. Marie Tempest talked at one time of wanting to undertake it, but decided it was too unsympathetic for her. The role was played in America by Mrs. Leslie Carter. Mrs. Campbell, meeting her at a party, said, "Oh, how do you do? I thought you were dead." The character needs to be faded and somewhat grotesque, but it is a brilliant and amusing part, and, though the love scenes of the young people are very dated now, I am still inclined to think it Maugham's best play. Aynesworth played Lord Porteous in the original production and also in a revival some years later. John Drew played the part in America.

5

NEW YORK

I have always loved cities—first London, where I was born and lived throughout my boyhood, then Oxford, New York, and Venice, in that order. I had always longed to work in America, and it has never disappointed me, from the first time I came here, so long ago, in 1928, to act in a play which only ran a week.

Luckily, however, before I went back home (since I could not, at that time, afford to stay) I saw something of the Broadway theatre, flourishing and lively as it was in those days—Helen Hayes in *Coquette,* Judith Anderson in *Behold the Bridegroom,* and, standing at the back of the orchestra in the new Ziegfeld Theatre among a packed matinée audience, I watched with rapture the original production of *Show Boat,* with Norma Terris, Howard Marsh, Charles Winninger, Jules Bledsoe, Edna May Oliver, and, best of all, Helen Morgan as Julie singing "Bill" on the top of a piano with a long chiffon handkerchief dangling from her wrist. Mabel Mercer was at Tony's in 52nd Street and there were speak-easies, the Cotton Club, evenings in Harlem, the dining room at the Hotel Algonquin packed with celebrities, and unexpected meetings with English players I knew who were acting in New York. No wonder I have always vividly remembered that first short visit with wonder and delight. Today, after living here very often over many years, I am still stimulated by the unpredictable, electric, liveliness of the city, despite the extremes of heat and cold, cramped taxis, and sweltering buses, the squalor of the subways, the steamheating, and air conditioning, the friendliness and politeness (as well as the occasional rudeness), the foreignness mixed with familiarity. I love the brilliant quality of the New York lights, twinkling towers as they begin to glitter on Central Park South round six o'clock on a winter evening—the strip of sky which one can always see in four directions even from the deep canyons of the avenues. The vista of Fifth Avenue from St. Patrick's Cathedral to the Plaza Hotel is, to me, one of the finest sights in the world, with an elegance that our own Bond Street used once to have but has now lost forever, smothered as it is today by so many cheap new shops and unimaginative modern buildings.

American theatres dismayed me at first with their extreme width of auditorium and shallow stages—no bars or proper lounges (save for those cavernous overheated cellars, with queues lining up for the telephone in the intermissions) and the disagreeable men who tear up one's tickets as one passes through the doors in the narrow entrance halls. Yet the sense of expectation in an American audience—especially at matinées when the women predominate, screaming and waving greetings to one another across the aisles, and wildly applauding every entrance and exit, song or dance—is wonderfully infectious and finally rewarding, both for actors and spectators alike, and infinitely preferable to the scene in London, where trays of tea are shuffled in and out over people's heads, and the elderly ladies sit munching with dogged indifference, often slumbering and even snoring as the afternoon wears on.

I have, alas, no memories of seeing the great actors and actresses of America as I have of so many in England, though Guthrie McClintic used to entertain me with wonderful stories of Mrs. Fiske and Emily Stevens, Nazimova and Laurette Taylor, all alas before my time.

PAULINE LORD, JOHN BARRYMORE, JANE COWL

I happened to be present on the first night of a new play *Salvation* by Sidney Howard at the Empire Theatre in New York when I first appeared there in *The Patriot* in 1928. I remember little of the play save a splendid performance by Osgood Perkins, as a newspaperman, and the strange broken syllables and emotional power of Pauline Lord, who played the leading part.

I had seen her once before at the Strand Theatre in London (also, oddly enough, on the opening night) when she played O'Neill's *Anna Christie* and took the town by storm. But when Greta Garbo made her huge success in the film version of the play, Pauline Lord's wonder acting was soon forgotten, though not by me. Years later, I was leaving the Plaza Hotel in New York by a side door one afternoon, when I recognized Miss Lord, sitting in an armchair in the passageway, looking extremely sad and lonely. I ventured to introduce myself, and her face lit up with pleasure when I reminded her of her triumph in London. But she told me she had lost heart for the theatre and had just returned from playing Amanda (the mother) in a tour of Tennessee Williams's *The Glass Menagerie,* which I imagine she must have acted brilliantly, though eclipsed, I suppose, as far as New York was concerned at any rate, by comparison with the great Laurette Taylor who created the part on Broadway, an actress whom, alas, I never saw. Pauline Lord's pathos was extraordinary, individual and evocative, and I always think of her strange beauty on the stage.

I greatly admired John Barrymore as Hamlet when I saw him in London in 1926, and once heard him speak at a Sunday Dinner Club, but I never met him, though he sent me a page-long telegram when I was honoured ten years later at a dinner in New York by the Players Club. His famous sister Ethel I met several times at George Cukor's house in Beverly Hills in her last years, but I never saw her act except on the screen.

Jane Cowl I met in London and saw her when she played Noël Coward's *Easy Virtue* there in 1926. Miss Cowl was most effective in the Coward play, and adapted her acting style to great advantage in modern plays after successes in New York both as Juliet and Cleopatra. She was also very dramatic in private life. She fainted one night when she was in the audience watching John Barrymore in Galsworthy's *Justice.* A few weeks later someone told Barrymore "Jane Cowl is in front again." "Is she?" Barrymore remarked airily. "I do hope she'll give a good performance."

While she was in England, Miss Cowl wrote a play under the pen name C. R. Avery entitled *Hervey House.* It was presented at His Majesty's Theatre in May 1935, with an all-star cast headed by Fay Compton and Gertrude Lawrence. (I was nearly in the play myself in the role eventually played by

Nicholas Hannen.) Margaret Rutherford made one of her first successes in a supporting part, as did Alan Webb, but *Hervey House* did not achieve a long run although it was brilliantly directed by Tyrone Guthrie. During the weeks they were awaiting rehearsals, Fay Compton and Gertrude Lawrence made a tour of Devonshire riding bicycles, while a Rolls-Royce followed them distantly in case they became tired.

LESLIE HOWARD

The year 1936 when I played Hamlet at the Empire Theatre in New York for Guthrie McClintic (with Lillian Gish, Judith Anderson, and Arthur Byron) was, of course, one of the most exciting of my life, though I was placed in a somewhat embarrassing position when Leslie Howard appeared during the same season in his own production and with a number of English players in his cast. (Malcolm Keen and Harry Andrews who played the King and Horatio respectively were the only English actors in mine.)

Howard had announced that he had decided not to put on the play before I had agreed to come over in the spring of that year, but later changed his mind, and I was upset at having to compete with a fellow countryman whom I did not know but greatly admired, and who was also an internationally popular film star. The reviews for my performance were encouraging but not wholly enthusiastic, and I was expecting a run of not more than a few weeks. When Howard opened, however, a few weeks later and was poorly received, our performances began to sell out almost immediately. The press tried to persuade us to meet and give interviews about one another, but we stuck to our own guns and behaved with as much dignity as possible, still the Battle of the Hamlets was quite a popular topic in the city for several months. Beatrice Lillie played in a sketch about us in a revue, and even the taxi drivers used to ask which of the Hamlets I was when I directed them to the stage door of the Empire. The abdication of the Duke of Windsor which happened at the same time, helped to fascinate the New York public with England and Royalty, everyone arguing and taking sides.

I have been lucky enough, through my work in the theatre, to meet four American Presidents. Lillian Gish took me to see President and Mrs. Roosevelt at the White House, and I met Truman, Johnson, and Kennedy on different occasions when they came to see plays that I was appearing in. During the *Hamlet* run I did not keep a diary, and find it hard to remember the many fascinating and illustrious visitors who were kind enough to come round to see me.

But two amusing incidents have always remained with me. One night, when I was very tired at the end of two performances, Maria Ouspenskaya, an elderly Russian actress, was announced. I had greatly admired her in films, particularly *Dodsworth* and *The Rains Came,* and she had recently been acting in the theatre in New York in a Greek tragedy, though I had not been fortunate enough to see it. She came into the dressing room a formidable and striking personality with a long cigarette holder in her hand, looking very distinguished and escorted by an elegant young man who leaned gracefully against the wall behind her. "Oh, Madame Ouspenskaya," I burst out, gathering my dressing gown about me and wondering if I ought to kiss her hand, "I am so sorry to think you were in front tonight. I was dreadfully tired and I know I played so badly!" On which Madame nodded her head twice in profound approval, turned around, and left the room without a word.

On another evening, Judith Anderson brought in a friend of hers to see me, a Swedish Countess beautifully bejewelled and dressed. She seemed greatly moved by the performance and, as she was leaving, murmured, "I would like to give you something in remembrance of this great experience," and, putting out her hand, began to take off a most beautiful square cut emerald ring that she was wearing. I nervously began to put out my own hand, but, just as I did so, she hastily drew her ring back on to her finger and made a graceful exit. I thought I must have imagined the whole episode, but Judith Anderson assured me afterwards that it was perfectly true.

The generosity of the leading players in America has always charmed me. When I opened in *Hamlet* I received telegrams of good wishes from a number of stars whom I had never even met, and on the last night, Helen Hayes, who was playing *Victoria Regina* so brilliantly at the Broadhurst Theatre just four blocks from the Empire, sent over a tray with a bottle of champagne and glasses saying how sorry she was that I was leaving this neighbourhood. I have the happiest memories of the Players Club, the courtesy of its late presidents, Walter Hampden, Howard Lindsay, and Dennis King, and the dinners given there for me, and on other occasions for Alfred Lunt and Lynn Fontanne, and for Howard Lindsay just before his death. I was given a degree a few years ago at Brandeis University in Massachusetts and made a freeman of the City of Philadelphia, and I need hardly say that I have always found America, and Hollywood too—on the few occasions I have worked there—to be immensely kind and encouraging. I shall always look on this country as my second home, where I have made so many delightful friends among my fellow players and the audiences for whom I have played.

VIVIEN LEIGH

"What seems to me most remarkable, as far as her career was concerned, was her steady determination to be a fine stage actress, to make her career in the living theatre, when, with her natural beauty, skill, and grace of movement, gifts which were of course invaluable in helping to create the magic of her personality, she could so easily have stayed aloof and supreme in her unique position as a screen actress. Of course she will always be remembered as Scarlett O'Hara, as Lady Hamilton, and later for her wonderful acting in the *Streetcar* film. But these screen successes by no means satisfied her ambitions, and she had a lifelong devotion to the theatre, and determined to work there diligently through the years in order to reach the heights which she afterwards achieved. Though in her first big success, *The Mask of Virtue,* she had taken the critics and public by storm, she knew that her youth and beauty were the chief factors of her immediate success, and she was modest and shrewd enough to face the challenge of developing herself so as to find the widest possible range of which she was capable.

"Her marriage to Laurence Olivier was an inspiration to her qualities—not only as a devoted pupil but also as a brilliant partner. Her performance in their seasons together, not only at the St. James's Theatre (whose untimely destruction she tried so gallantly to prevent), but also at the Old Vic and Stratford, and in tours all over the world—in Russia, Australia, Europe and America fresh laurels were added to her crown. Besides the classic parts, she delighted everyone too in the modern plays she chose, each of which made different demands upon her versatility—*The Skin of Our Teeth, The Sleeping Prince, Antigone,* and later *Duel of Angels.*

"She had a charmingly distinctive voice. On the telephone one recognised it immediately—that touch of imperiousness, combined with a childlike eager warmth full of friendliness and gaiety. But she was determined to increase the range of it for the theatre, and in Shakespeare's Cleopatra, in which I thought she gave her finest classical performance, she succeeded in lowering her whole register from the natural pitch she was using as the little girl Cleopatra in Shaw's play—a remarkable feat which few actresses could have sustained as successfully as she did. Her Lady Macbeth, too, showed an astonishing vocal power and poignancy of feeling—and it is a thousand pities that the project of filming her performance of this was abandoned, for I believe it would have created worldwide admiration.

"Her manners both in the theatre and in private life were always impeccable. She was punctual, modest, and endlessly thoughtful and considerate. She was frank without being unkind, elegant but never ostentatious. Her houses were as lovely as her beautiful and simple clothes. Whenever she was not entirely absorbed in the theatre she was endlessly busy, decorating her rooms, planning surprises for her friends, giving advice on her garden, entertaining lavishly but always with the utmost grace and selectivity.

"I had never thought to become an intimate friend of hers. My first meeting with her was at Oxford in 1937, when she played the little queen in *Richard the Second* with the students. I was acting in London at the time, and so only met her when I was directing the rehearsals. The part is not a very interesting one, though she managed to endow it with every possible grace of speech and movement, and wore her mediaeval costumes with consummate charm—but I never got to know her in these days.

"A few years later, during the war, I acted with her in *The*

Doctor's Dilemma, when another actor was taken ill, and from that time we began an acquaintanceship which slowly ripened into a deep friendship and affection, and it is a wonderful happiness to me that during her last years I had the joy of seeing her so often and came to love her so well.

"Of course she was restless and drove herself too hard. Although she seemed so astonishingly resilient, she often suffered ill health and fits of great depression, but she made light of the fact and rarely admitted to it or talked about it to other people. Her courage in the face of personal unhappiness was touching and remarkable. She always spoke affectionately of those who had first recognised her talents and helped her to develop her natural gifts. She studied and experimented continually and always brought to rehearsal a willingness and technical flexibility which was the result of unceasing self-criticism and devotion to her work.

"As she grew older she acquired a new kind of beauty, without any need of artifice, and she seemed to harbour no resentment against the competition of younger beautiful women. She was always enormously interested in everything, people, places, changes of fashion—and she had friends of every different sort and kind in London, in her country homes and in America and Australia. How delightfully she would talk of her Japanese admirers, who wrote her such charmingly phrased letters, and of those in Russia, where her film *Waterloo Bridge* is still considered a classic. She had the most punctilious and gracious way of answering letters and of dealing with strangers, admirers, newspaper men and women, and she was loved in the theatres she worked in for her sweetness to staff and company alike.

"Her magic quality was unique. A great beauty, a natural star, a consummate screen actress and a versatile and powerful personality in the theatre—she had a range that could stretch from the comedy Sabina in *Skin of Our Teeth* to the naturalistic agonies of Blanche DuBois in *Streetcar,* and the major demands of Lady Macbeth and Cleopatra. Even in *Titus Andronicus,* when she had only a few short scenes, she contrived the most beautiful pictorial effects. Who can forget the macabre grace with which she guided the staff with her elbows to write in the sand with it, a ravished victim gliding across the stage in her long grey robe.

"We who loved her must be always thankful for knowing her and working with her, and salute her for all she gave the world, so generously and so gaily.

> Now boast thee, Death, in thy possession lies
> A lass unparallel'd."

6

SOME NON-ACTING ACTORS

SIR CHARLES HAWTREY, ALLAN AYNESWORTH, GERALD DU MAURIER, RONALD SQUIRE, AND A. E. MATTHEWS

Smart drawing-room comedy has always been staple fare in the London theatre, and Max Beerbohm, in one of his theatre notices of the early 1900s, writes mockingly of the absurdly overtailored "mimes" (as he always called the actors) with their impeccable trouserings with knife-edged creases and their overpolished hats and boots. But there were a number of fine players of that generation who could carry off their contemporary clothes with a more natural air.

Gerald du Maurier, for instance, used to wear old suits on the stage that were beautifully cut, but had obviously hung in his wardrobe for years. How fascinating he was, to men as well as women, although he was not at all conventionally handsome. He could slouch and lounge and flick his leading lady behind one ear as he played a love-scene, never seeming to raise his voice or force an emotion, yet he could be infinitely touching too without being in the least sentimental. His drunken painter, Dearth, in *Dear Brutus* was a masterpiece of understatement, acted with a mixture of infinite charm and regretful pathos. He could be flippant in light comedy or casually efficient in plays like *Raffles* and *Bulldog Drummond*. His technique was inimitably resourceful, though so well concealed. In one of his late successes, *Interference,* a drama by Roland Pertwee and Harold Deardon, he held the audience enthralled while he examined a murdered man's body in a long scene lasting several silent minutes, and once, when he played a silent valet at a charity matinée he managed to make an effective moment as he took the overcoat from the shoulders of one of the principal characters.

Charles Hawtrey and Allan Aynesworth belonged to the same naturalistic school as du Maurier, and, after their deaths Ronald Squire and A. E. Matthews continued the same kind of tradition on similar lines though they never achieved quite so much success.

Hawtrey and Aynesworth were both portly and well fed, looking more like businessmen than actors. They wore dark suits for formal occasions, their tweeds or riding breeches for the country were unobtrusively well cut, and their coats were roomy with big flapped pockets. They wore fancy waistcoats, gold watch-chains, and smart boots, and everything they did on the stage was perfect, so perfect that they did not seem to be acting at all. But of course they never experimented far from their own brilliant but limited range. One could never imagine them playing in Ibsen, Chekhov, Shakespeare, Sheridan, or Congreve. They might simply have strolled in for an hour or two for a little exercise as a change from sitting in their clubs. In a period when other actors took hours making up their faces, whether as juveniles or heavily disguised character-men, their faces looked more natural than anyone else's on the stage. And yet I believe they might have been equally distinguished if they had ventured into more ambitious fields.

At the end of his career, when he was past eighty, Aynesworth played Lord Conyngham in the opening scene of Laurence Housman's *Victoria Regina,* and partnered by my aunt, Mabel Terry-Lewis, whose distinction of bearing and diction were equal to his own, acted with a period style that put the rest of the cast to shame. And I remember meeting him once on the stone stairs at the back of the Coliseum where there was a gala matinée of *Drake,* dressed improbably as the Archbishop of Canterbury. In his robes and mitre, he looked magnificently authentic and not in the least ridiculous. But his dignified, witty approach to contemporary characters fitted his manner and personality to perfection and there were always new light comedies, however trivial, with parts in them to suit him. He was as solemnly humorous as the butler in Milne's *The Dover Road,* one thumb tucked slyly into a waistcoat pocket, as in playing the lovable monster Lord Porteous in Maugham's *The Circle,* fulminating as he lost his temper and his false teeth over the bridge table. How delighted he must have been when he created Algy in *The Importance of Being Earnest.* He had just the right kind of urbane flippancy, so hard to achieve for the young actors of today, especially in the second act—the Piccadilly dandy Bunburying in the country.

Sir George Alexander, of course, created the part of John Worthing in the original production. I have been told, however, that Wilde first intended the play for Hawtrey, and took it round to the theatre where he was acting at the time demanding a sum down immediately. Hawtrey, usually as hard-up and extravagant as Wilde himself, sent round to the box office asking them to advance the money, but this they refused to do, on which Wilde went off to the St. James's

Theatre round the corner and sold the play to Alexander.
Hawtrey had created the part of Lord Goring in Wilde's *An
Ideal Husband* at the Haymarket some years before, and I
have always been deeply shocked to read how he and Charles
Brookfield—who played Goring's valet in the same production—had rounded up a number of the more sordid witnesses
who appeared for Queensberry in the famous libel action. The
two men gave a supper party together to celebrate Wilde's
sentence in 1895, when, of course, the enormously successful
first production of *The Importance* had to be so suddenly
taken off.

Whether Hawtrey (as well as Brookfield) had always hated
Wilde is not on record, but he would certainly have been ideal
casting for the part of Worthing. No one could tell a lie on the
stage with more superb conviction, and his scene of mourning
for his lost brother would have been the very kind of thing he
always did best. I was lucky enough to see him in a number of
plays, *The Naughty Wife* with Gladys Cooper, a revival of
Maugham's *Jack Straw,* with Lottie Venne (a tiny, brilliant
farceuse whom I also adored), and in *Ambrose Applejohn's
Adventure* by Walter Hackett, in which he was enormously
funny, wearing an eighteenth-century pirate costume (in
some kind of dream or fantasy scene) and using comic oaths,
swaggering about without the slightest appearance of knowing
how absurd he was. In Maugham's First War light comedy,
Home and Beauty, he played the husband of the feather-
headed young wife (Gladys Cooper) who, imagining him
killed in battle, has rashly married again. Hawtrey entered a
clumsy reach-me-down suit which was immediately funny on
his large figure, and discovering a baby in the nurse's arms, suddenly realized what had happened in his absence and brought
down the curtain (and the house) with the line, "Hell, said
the Duchess!" And I can see him now trying to cook a ra-

tioned meal on the kitchen range with the help of the second husband, exquisitely polite in his exchanges with the spinster-ish professional co-respondent whom he has called in to ar-range a belated divorce—Jean Cadell at her most acidly re-spectable.

A great gambler and *bon viveur* in private life, Hawtrey achieved the same airy effect of enjoyment and leisure when he acted, passing off an embarrassing situation, eating a stage meal, or galvanizing undistinguished dialogue. In his perform-ances, as with Aynesworth's, stylishness and ease were apparent in everything he did. Entrances, exits, and stage crosses never seemed planned or theatrical, they simply seemed to happen. Diction, phrasing, and timing had been studied, practised, and then concealed, so that dialogue appeared to be completely spontaneous. Both players were solid British gentlemen, Lon-doners to their fingertips. The moment they appeared on the stage one sank back comfortably in one's seat. The silk would never be creased, the wheels would revolve with infallible pre-cision. What masters of their craft they were, and how per-fectly they executed it!

Ronald Squire had often understudied Hawtrey and fol-lowed his methods to great effect. He used a very subtle throw-away technique, with his own particular distinction of per-sonality and deadpan comedy timing. In *By Candle Light*, Lonsdale's *The Last of Mrs. Cheyney*, and *On Approval*, he was the aristocratic *flâneur* or the perfect butler to his finger-tips, and in Maugham's *The Breadwinner* his rebellious stock-broker paterfamilias was equally delightful. But he also gave an unexpectedly skilful performance as the Doctor in *A Month in the Country*, with Valerie Taylor and Michael Redgrave, and would I am sure have been equally enchanting as Gaev in *The Cherry Orchard*, which he was rehearsing when the Second War broke out and the production (by Michel St. Denis) had to be abandoned.

I once flew with him to Hollywood in 1952 when I was to act Cassius for M.G.M. in *Julius Caesar,* and he was to play a supporting part in a film with Olivia de Havilland and Richard Burton at another studio. I was much embarrassed to find that, while he was greeted with scant ceremony, the red carpet was rolled out for me. I was delighted, however, to hear that, after two days' shooting, the crew working with him had become immediately aware of his unique talents and distinction, and treated him as an important star, though he always loved to pretend, as did many others of the du Maurier school, that the theatre was only a chore to be endured as a means of making money as opposed to the more pleasurable diversions of golf, the race-course, or the club.

A. E. Matthews outlived the other four players by several years, and was still appearing, both in film studios and in the theatre, when he was past ninety. As a young man he had been an attractive juvenile, playing in *Peter's Mother* by Mrs. Henry de la Pasture with Marion Terry and in *Alice Sit by the Fire* with Ellen, and in America he created Aynesworth's part of Algy in *The Importance of Being Earnest.* I first saw him, during the First War, as the leading man in the famous *Peg O' My Heart,* Laurette Taylor's great success written by her husband J. Hartley Manners. She herself had left the cast after a few months, and Mary O'Farrell—afterwards famous as a radio actress—had now taken over the part of Peg, entering with a shaggy dog in her arms and a cardboard box for luggage. My eldest brother was in love with her at the time and took me in the pit one night to see the play. As Matthews entered he whispered, "That is the oldest juvenile in London," (a remark which I remembered somewhat ruefully a few years ago when I was probably the oldest Joseph Surface on record). In later life, Matthews looked like a grumpy bloodhound, with mulberry cheeks and pale watery eyes. He appeared, both on and off the stage, in an amazing collection of Edwardian clothes, jodhpurs, hacking jackets, tweed suits with check patterns and narrow turned-up trousers, and squashed shapeless hats.

He learned his lines very sketchily (and improvised and gagged brilliantly when he forgot them) but he had a delightful cheeky nonchalance and a solid basis of technique which always made him a delight to watch. I directed him once in a play and we got on together very well at the rehearsals. Meeting him in the street some time afterwards I asked him where he was going. "To the Garrick Club," he replied, and then, quick as a flash, seeing by the look in my eye that I was not yet a member of that august fellowship, added, "I like the lavatories there so much. They have handles at the sides that help you to pull yourself up!" *The Chiltern Hundreds,* by William Douglas Home, in which he acted very late in his career was an enormous success. It opened in London in 1947 and ran for 651 performances. Matthews dozed one night in his dressing-room and fell off his chair on to the floor where he proceeded to continue his nap unperturbed. The call boy, finding him there, was terrified and rushed to the stage manager crying, "Mr. Matthews is dead," but before the understudy could be sent for the actor had woken up and strolled to his entrance as if nothing unusual had happened. Later he summoned the boy to his room and said to him, "Next time you find me on the floor I suggest you tell them, 'I *think* Mr. Matthews is dead.'"

He created quite a furore in the press when he staged a sit-down strike, with rugs, pillows, and a shooting-stick, outside his house in protest against a hideous new lamp post that was to be erected there. The last time I saw him, at a supper party, he arrived late as he was still acting in the theatre. He consumed a large supper, with a quantity of gin and several glasses of wine, and then, apparently perfectly sober, toddled off to appear in a location shot for a film to be taken at some suburban tube station at two o'clock in the morning.

Of these five comedians, Charles Hawtrey was undoubtedly the most brilliant. Both he and du Maurier were also skilled directors, both of men and women, though I think neither of them ever directed a classic play. But they were the undoubted masters of a school that achieved an enormously high standard during the first twenty years of the century, a standard founded, no doubt, on the productions of the Kendals and the Bancrofts before both couples retired (enormously rich and successful) in early middle age.

Hawtrey and du Maurier, despite their many years of prosperity, spent generously and lavishly, and needed to continue working to the end of their lives, unable to afford to leave the stage when they began to tire. The first successes of Noël Coward, in 1924, must have shaken their confidence considerably, much in the same way as my own acting generation was shaken by the new school of Angry Young Men in 1956. Coward himself had begun his stage career with Hawtrey, and always acknowledged gratefully what he learned from him. Du Maurier trained a number of brilliant players who were to gain important positions in the theatre after his death, but he was suspicious of young highbrows, and only became fond of Coward and Charles Laughton when he met them, in his last years, and was won over by their personal charm. I think he seldom cared to see other productions than his own, and was fearful of being displaced, not realizing how enormously he was respected and admired by all the young players who were beginning to be successful in the theatre.

Haidée Wright in *Milestones*
at the Royalty Theatre, 1912

I went round to see her after
she had played a French peasant mother in a melodrama.
At the climax of the play she
had to shoot her own son—an
intense, electrifying scene.
When I attempted to congratu-
late her on the power of her
performance, she merely shook
her head and murmured in her
curious, bleating voice, "Oh I
thought it was just a little
thing that would be blown
away by the wind!"

Haidée Wright and Robert
Loraine in *The Father* at the
Everyman Theatre,
Hampstead, 1927

Another great performance of
hers, heartbreaking in its
tragic intensity, was as the old
nurse in Strindberg's *The
Father*. She complained bitterly
to me of Loraine's violence in
playing this scene, which he
would insist on rehearsing
with painfully physical realism
at the end of each performance, when she was longing
to get home.

Ada King in *The Queen Was in the Parlour*
at St. Martin's Theatre, 1926

She was supposed never to be able to appear in evening dress, because her dead husband's name (Henry) was tattooed across her chest. After she retired from the stage, Dame May Whitty and Dame Sybil Thorndike, who were both fond of her, took care to pay her little attentions from time to time with presents and remembrances. Knowing she was fond of white wine, Dame Sybil sent her some for Christmas. "Two of the bottles were broken," she wrote back in acknowledgement, "and it was the wrong vintage. It was kind of you, all the same."

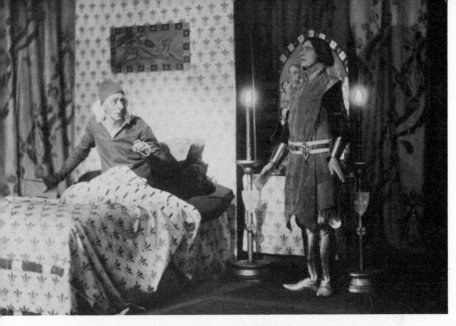

Ernest Thesiger and Sybil Thorndike in *Saint Joan* at the New Theatre, 1924

As a very inexperienced Romeo, I had appeared aged only nineteen, (with Gwen Ffrangcon-Davies playing Juliet) in a not very successful revival of Shakespeare's tragedy, at an unfashionable theatre in North London. We were invited by a rich Dutch lady to perform the Balcony Scene one Sunday evening, in the garden of her country house, at a party she was giving for some distinguished friends.

On arriving, I was somewhat intimidated to find Thesiger (whom I already knew slightly through my parents) sitting on the lawn, eating cherries from a straw hat, Lydia Lopokova, the famous Diaghilev ballerina (who later married Maynard Keynes, the economist) was sitting by his side, while Mrs. Violet Gordon-Woodhouse sat at a clavichord, just inside the drawing-room windows, playing Couperin and Bach. Having dressed and made ourselves up, Gwen and I proceeded to give a very uncertain open-air performance. Our wigs and costumes looked very false in the real moonlight, and I had to risk life and limb on a rickety espalier below an uncomfortably high balcony on the side of the house. Gnats and midges hovered and buzzed in the night air, and at intervals we could hear our intrepid hostess, murmuring, in her strong Dutch accent, "Oh! It's so [slap] romantic!"

Unaccustomed to the correct behaviour on such a private occasion, we accepted gratefully the compliments bestowed on us at the end of the evening, as well as a briefcase (for me) and some lady trifles for Gwen, as presents from our hostess. As we were leaving, Ernest Thesiger suddenly emerged from the shadows, nudged my elbow, and remarked in a sepulchral voice, "I do hope you were both given *enormous* cheques."

Robert Farquharson in *The Cenci* at the New Theatre, 1922

He stammered badly off the stage, but once he had learned a part (or could even read it in a radio studio), he was an immensely skilful vocalist. Like Somerset Maugham, he knew how to embarrass one or keep one in suspense if one caught him unawares with a remark, and I always had a sneaking feeling the both men had grown to use their disability with considerable skill if they wished to embarrass or discomfort someone in conversation.

Farquharson was reputed to have dealings with the black arts. Once, when he was playing Cardinal Wolsey, the young page, kneeling before him with a basin for the Cardinal to wash his hands, lost his balance and spilled some water over his scarlet robe. Farquharson spat during his next speech, and the boy was spattered with his saliva. As the young actor left the stage he felt blood flowing on his upper lip, and found when he looked in the glass in his dressing-room that he was bleeding profusely. The young actor vouched for this story and told it to me himself.

7

TWO SPLENDID CHARACTER ACTRESSES

ADA KING AND HAIDÉE WRIGHT

Neither of these two players would have made a fortune by their looks, and neither was ever a great popular star in the commercial sense of the word, but both showed immense distinction in any part I ever saw them play.

ADA KING

Ada King had created the part of Mrs. Jones, the charwoman, in Galsworthy's play, *The Silver Box,* as a member of Miss Horniman's famous company at the Gaiety Theatre in Manchester, and among her colleagues were Basil Dean (as stage manager as well as actor), Sybil Thorndike, and Lewis Casson. When I was on tour there in the 1940s I happened to notice a delightful photograph still on display in a pub window opposite the Theatre Royal, showing the whole company grouped together, and I thought of asking if I might buy it, but of course when I was in Manchester a year or two later the pub had disappeared forever and the photograph as well.

Ada King was short and red-faced, with sandy hair, wearing gold rimmed pince-nez on her large turned-up nose when she was not on the stage. During the early Twenties, Basil Dean engaged her for several of his productions at the St. Martin's Theatre under his ReanDean management, and it was in *R.U.R.,* the Robot play by the Czech brothers Capek, that I saw her for the first time. She played a housekeeper, and in one scene she impressed me greatly as she rushed across the stage crying out some Biblical-sounding speech of impending doom, as Leslie Banks, terrifyingly grotesque in a kind of spaceman's uniform and helmet, climbed in through the windows at the back of the stage. I next saw her in a comic part, an old biddy sitting on the steps of her slum house, in a play by Charles McEvoy, *The Likes of 'Er.* In this play she acted with Mary Clare and the young Hermione Baddeley, who made her first big success as a violent cockney child who smashed up the stage at the climax of the play, hurling china in all directions.

Ada King was as effective in costume as in modern dress. Her performance as Roxane's duenna in Robert Loraine's production of *Cyrano de Bergerac* (presented by Cochran and decorated by Edmond Dulac, whose fairybook illustrations had meant so much to me when I was a boy) was a delicious thumbnail sketch. Wearing a jaunty little hat with a long feather, she might have stepped straight out of an etching by Callot, while in the Thorndike-Casson *Henry the Eighth* at the Empire, she was pure Holbein, inimitable as the Old Lady gossiping to Anne Boleyn. Pathos and broad comedy seemed to be equally within her range, and I admired her in *The Way Things Happen* by Clemence Dane at the Ambassadors Theatre, and in Noël Coward's *The Queen Was in the*

Parlour at the St. Martin's, a Ruritanian melodrama in which Madge Titheradge starred with Herbert Marshall, Lady Tree, and Francis Lister. In one scene Ada King, playing the secretary of the romantic Queen, got an enormous laugh as she tiptoed back into the throne-room she had just left and murmured, "Oh, my umbrella."

One day I instantly recognized her as I passed her in the street. She had on her gold pince-nez, and a little furpiece was round her neck, with a sad little fox's mask clasping it together and hanging down on to her chest, like the woman in one of Katherine Mansfield's short stories. I could not resist going up to her and thanking her for the pleasure her acting had always given me, and she seemed gratified but extremely shy. Some months afterwards, when Emlyn Williams and I were going into management to act in and direct together a play he had written, we were at a loss to cast the part of an eccentric Countess, and I suddenly thought of Ada King, who had not appeared on the stage for a considerable time. We wrote to her and sent her the script, asking her to come and see us as soon as she had read it, and she arrived punctually next day at the Queen's Theatre, where we met her in the foyer. She looked much the same as ever, still the pince-nez and the fur necklet and the odd old-fashioned clothes. She sat down with us, saying she was flattered to think she should be remembered by such young men, and that she liked the part we had suggested for her. "But," she added firmly, "my memory is no longer as good as it once was, and I am afraid I could not dream of accepting an engagement nowadays unless I had several weeks beforehand to study and memorize my lines." Then she gathered up her bag and her umbrella, shook hands with us both, and stepped briskly out into Shaftesbury Avenue. It was a most touching little interview. I never saw her again.

HAIDÉE WRIGHT

Haidée Wright was also in *The Way Things Happen,* and she had, I remember, a scene with Ada King in which, like the Lion and the Unicorn, each appeared to be fighting for the crown. If Ada King emerged the winner on this occasion it may have been either because her lines were better or because she was extremely funny. Also she was more real, or seemed to be so, though she had not the sheer power of Haidée Wright's taut theatrical temperament. A tiny figure—head erect, ramrod back, and flashing eyes—one could hardly conceive of anything less funny than the acting of Haidée Wright. Like Geneviève Ward (whom I once saw in *The Aristocrat* with George Alexander), she knew how to dominate the stage with absolute authority in what my father always described as The Grand Manner.

It was to her that I wrote my first fan letter to an actress when I was still a schoolboy, after seeing her in a revival of *Milestones.* I said in the letter that I had cried my eyes out, and signed it J. Gielgud. I was somewhat saddened to receive a gracious reply addressed to Miss J. Gielgud! The play, by Arnold Bennett and Edward Knoblock, is the drama of a family whose various members appear in the successive episodes at three separate periods in their lives. Haidée Wright was the spinster aunt, thwarted in early life through some passionate romantic attachment which had gone wrong. Halfway through the play she had a dramatic outburst, dressed in a Victorian bonnet and a dress with a bustle, and carrying a tiny folded parasol in the crook of her arm. In the last act she entered leaning on a cane, and later played her final scene crouched in a low chair before the fire, dressed in a long grey satin gown, with a shawl over her shoulders and a lace cap on her white hair.

She was very moving in the tiny part of the Abbess in the Convent scene of *Cyrano* (again in the same company as Ada King, though in this play they did not meet) and soon afterwards I sat in the gallery to watch her first-night triumph as Queen Elizabeth in Clemence Dane's ill-fated and unequal play *Will Shakespeare*. Her stature might have seemed more appropriate to Queen Victoria, but her performance immediately dismissed any such thought from one's mind. She moved with consummate dignity and grace, wearing her fine costumes superbly and delivering her speeches—the best in the play—in thrilling tones. She was to play Elizabeth again in *The Dark Lady of the Sonnets* some years later, and in Shaw's slight but witty sketch she drew a different portrait of the same woman, an admirable contrast of sly vanity and patriotic fervour.

Another great performance of hers, heartbreaking in its tragic intensity, was as the old nurse in Strindberg's *The Father* in which she had to put her master into a straitjacket, coaxing him with familiar words as if he were still a child.

She could make an enormous effect with a single line, as she did in *The Unknown,* a spiritualistic play by Somerset Maugham, which I was not lucky enough to see, when she cried out, "Who is going to forgive God?" And in an undistinguished melodrama about Edmund Kean at Drury Lane, during a scene in the green room at the theatre, the double doors at the back of the stage were suddenly thrown open and "Mrs. Garrick" was announced. Haidée Wright, in a dark dress and simple bonnet entered, walking with an ebony stick, and moving down to H. A. Saintsbury, who was playing Kean, handed him a case which she was holding in her hand. As she opened it, she said very simply, "Mr. Kean, these are my husband's medals," and the whole audience sat spellbound and tearful, although the episode was quite unconnected with the rest of the play.

With American audiences she was equally popular. The part of the old actress, Fanny Cavendish, in *The Royal Family* (founded on the Barrymores by Edna Ferber and George S. Kaufman) was created in New York by Haidée Wright. In London the part was played by Marie Tempest, but I fancy that Haidée Wright's performance must have had a touch of the barnstormer which may have been broader and more colourful. Her voice, with its strange throbbing tremolo, became more mannered in her later years and it was easy to imitate her quavering tones. But I never liked to hear anyone make fun of her, and refused to go to see her in a stupid play, *The Aunt of England,* in which people said that she was beginning to caricature herself. When I came to know her personally I found that she suffered from poor health and a kind of persecution mania, complaining of being bullied by her directors and harassed by financial worries. "Dear Haidée Wright," said the witty Lady Tree. "Always so right, and never in her heyday."

She told me once that her greatest youthful ambition had been to play Juliet, for which of course she never had the looks. In her earliest days in the theatre she had acted a boy's part in Wilson Barrett's famous religious melodrama, *The Sign of the Cross,* and learned to give blood-curdling screams from offstage as she was being tortured, and she was a painted lady of uncertain age in Forbes-Robertson's greatest commercial success, *The Passing of the Third Floor Back,* a wildly sentimental piece by Jerome K. Jerome in which Christ, thinly concealed under the disguise of a character called "The Stranger," arrived to persuade the guests in a Bloomsbury lodging house to abjure their selfish ways.

She was, I suppose, somewhat old-fashioned in her acting by the time I saw her, and I must reluctantly admit that in two modern plays, *The Distaff Side* by John Van Druten, and a drama adapted from the French called *No Man's Land* (in which she was a peasant mother forced to shoot her own son at the climax of the play) she did seem to be rather too blatantly stagey to be entirely convincing. Why was she never given the opportunity, I wonder, to play Volumnia, Queen Margaret, or Hecuba? She would have been magnificent in such roles, for she needed tragedy—and how few tragedians, men or women, have we ever produced in the English theatre! —to display her emotional powers to the full. She had a great spirit in her little body, and the passionate intensity which she could always evoke, even with indifferent material, revealed an iron discipline and technique as striking in the actress as it was emotionally moving to the audience.

8

THREE BRILLIANT ECCENTRICS

ESMÉ PERCY, ERNEST THESIGER, AND ROBERT FARQUHARSON

They were all three very unusual in appearance for those days —dandified, flamboyant, fond of wearing jewellery and unconventional clothes. Thesiger was tall and angular, with a long turned-up nose of a most unusual shape, Farquharson thickset and slightly lame, with big pebble spectacles and reddish-gold hair which appeared to be dyed, a face which looked as if it were painted (and possibly was) and a congenital stammer which disappeared when he was acting. Esmé Percy, on the other hand, was short and plump, with a broken nose and only one eye, disabilities which must have been horribly painful to his vanity, but which he had learned to overcome by sheer force of personality and charm. He lost his eye just before the Second War, when he was attacked by a Great Dane he was stroking. The accident upset him terribly and he even contemplated suicide. But he always adored dogs and kept one with him to the end, although he had twice been seriously mauled by them. As a young man he had been a great beauty but I never heard him bitter at growing old and losing his looks. He even took it in good part, when, in *The Lady's Not for Burning,* in which he was inimitably funny as the drunken tinker in the last act, his false eye fell out on to the stage. We were all too dismayed to move, until one of the young men in the cast, who was also a doctor, managed to step forward and surreptitiously hand it back to him. Meanwhile Esmé was heard to murmur, "Don't step on it, for God's sake. They're so expensive!" After this episode, I suggested he might wear a black patch which suited the part very well, and somewhat reluctantly he agreed to do so. His sweetness over the affair was very typical. Sorting out some old letters written to me at various times about my acting, I found several from him which were among the most generous I ever received from a fellow-player.

He delighted in the company of young people, and when we took *The Lady* to America his enthusiasm was enchanting. Though already an elderly man, he would seek out the most interesting places to visit, had himself elected to several of the best clubs in Washington, Boston, and New York, to which he took me as his guest, and insisted on giving supper parties in Greenwich Village, at which all the youngsters sitting round him were fascinated by his stories and the amusing comments with which he embellished them.

His mother was French, and Esmé used to boast that he had been trained in Sarah Bernhardt's company, and that she had advised him to leave it because he was too much like her. He gave a wonderful lecture about her in which he imitated her voice to perfection.

His own vocal range was extraordinary. Once, during the war, broadcasting with me in a radio version of *Hamlet,* he acted three parts, the Ghost, the Player King, and Osric, using a different pitch and tone of course for each. He played a great deal of Shaw, and revelled in the elaborate speaking of Shavian prose, though he was also a somewhat inaccurate study and the prompter was apt to be a good deal in evidence during his performances. I saw him in the *The Shewing-up of Blanco Posnet,* and as Dubedat in *The Doctor's Dilemma* with Gwen Ffrangcon-Davies.

At the end of the First World War when he ran a theatre in Cologne for the British troops, he persuaded Mrs. Patrick Campbell to come out and appear with him in *Pygmalion,* when she proceeded to behave in her usual unpredictable fashion. Throughout the first act she kept muttering to Higgins, "Oh, do get on. Get on. You're so slow." In the second, as he tried to follow her instructions, she whispered, "Now you're gabbling, you know. You're much too fast." And in the third, while he tremblingly awaited the final onslaught, she gazed down sadly at his suede shoes (considered a very unmanly fashion in those far-off days), and remarked, shaking her head sadly as she turned to him with her back towards the audience. "Oh you're quite wrong. He's not that kind of man at all."

ERNEST THESIGER

Ernest Thesiger, too, was a splendid Shavian actor. His famous performance as the Dauphin in the original production of *Saint Joan,* with Sybil Thorndike, was definitive—an astonishing mixture of Gothic fantasy, brilliant comedy and underlying pathos. He later made successes in two other Shaw plays, *Geneva*—in which he wore an eyeglass and looked like Austen Chamberlain—and as Charles the Second in *In Good King Charles's Golden Days,* just before the Second War. During the Twenties, his ghillie in Barrie's *Mary Rose* failed to convince me, though he boasted of having taken long walks in Battersea Park with a real Scottish peasant whom he had hired to teach him the correct accent. But I thought he should never play anything but upper-class characters, though perhaps he might have been amusing as Malvolio, since he could appear very overweening when he chose. He was often waspish and sometimes malicious (though less so as he grew older) but he was also very courageous. He had joined up as a private soldier in the First War, refusing to take a commission, and was very popular with the other men, who were greatly impressed to see him sitting in a trench among them, busily engaged in doing needlework. His hands were badly scarred by shrapnel wounds, but he managed them admirably on the stage and was very proud of his hobbies, painting and petit-point. He was fond of collecting antiques and bibelots. These he would exhibit on a shelf in his dressing-room and would sometimes sell them to members of the company or give them as presents to his friends. He loved hobnobbing with Royalty, and liked to mention that Queen Mary and Princess Marie-Louise often showed a gracious interest in his work. He was thrifty about money and loved to sharpen his wit on that of his many witty contemporaries. He led the Men's Dress Reform League at one time, and championed shorts and more comfortable leisure clothes, swathing his neck in scarves fastened with jewelled pins long before they began to become a fashion. Somebody once asked him, "What do you say when you meet Nijinsky?" "Oh," replied Ernest gravely. "Say? You don't say anything. You just give him a pearl." It was said that he always wore a string of very good pearls round his own neck, and never took it off for fear that the loss of the warmth of his skin might spoil their quality. One night at the beginning of 1940 there was an air raid warning at Oxford, where he happened to be acting in a new play, and was staying at the Randolph Hotel. All the guests were ordered to go down to the basement shelter. Ernest created somewhat of a sensation, vividly dressed in Russian high-necked pyjamas and a spectacular dressing-gown, and sat bolt upright in a corner with his spectacles on his nose and a piece of embroidery in his hands. After a while the assembled company began to doze and he knew he was no longer attracting such conspicuous interest. Suddenly he clutched his throat and cried, "My God! My pearls! No, No, it's all right. I've got them on."

He played the first Witch for me in *Macbeth* during 1942, and was very effective and uncanny in the part. He had always a brilliant talent for female impersonation. One of the best scenes in Noël Coward's first big Cochran revue, *On With the Dance,* was a boarding house sketch in which Thesiger and Douglas Byng, as two old harridans, undressed as they made ready for bed. And I once saw him give an impersonation of Violet Vanbrugh, whose striking looks he managed to caricature most cleverly.

The last time he appeared in London we were together in an unsuccessful play, and I met him one day in the street shortly before we began rehearsing and said how glad I was that he had promised to undertake the part. "I think it is a splendid play," I said, "don't you?" "I'm afraid I don't," Ernest murmured darkly and went his way. I didn't dare to ask him why, in that case, he had agreed to accept the engagement, but during the short run he acted with his usual distinction and received quite an ovation from the audience at his entrance on the first night. But he was tiring fast, and I used to feel sad as I passed his open dressing-room door to see him lying on the sofa half asleep between his scenes. He was an extraordinary and rather touching character, an actor of unique imagination, with a most beautiful perfection of speech and period style.

ROBERT FARQUHARSON

Robert Farquharson's real name was Robin de la Condamine, and he was reputed to be a rich amateur with a background of Italian nobility. He acted with Tree at His Majesty's and I was surprised to find his name, along with those of Granville-Barker and Courtenay Thorpe, in the cast list of the copyright performance of *Caesar and Cleopatra* given by Mrs. Patrick Campbell in 1899, showing that he must have been touring with her at that time in some other play. I had often heard when I was a young man of his huge personal success as Herod in Wilde's *Salome,* given for a private performance, so when he came behind the scenes with a mutual friend after my extremely immature performance of Romeo to Gwen Ffrangcon-Davies's Juliet (I was then only nineteen years old) I was extremely flattered to hear him say, "You have taught me something about the part of Romeo I never knew before!" Unfortunately I boasted of the supposed compliment to the same mutual friend a few days later, and was shattered to be told, "Robin said it was the first time he had ever realized that Romeo could be played as Juliet."

It took a good many years for me to recover from this snub, and I was always slightly in awe of Farquharson whenever I happened to meet him. Once, standing in a crowded bus, he called out to me, peering through the heads and shoulders of the other passengers, "I'm just off to see my d-d-darling d-d-dentist!" Though his acting was vivid and original, I always found it slightly out of key with the rest of the productions in which he played. In *Such Men Are Dangerous,* an adaptation by Ashley Dukes of a German play, he appeared as the mad Emperor Paul the First. I had acted in New

York in the same play—then called *The Patriot* (with Lyn Harding, Leslie Faber and Madge Titheradge in the other leading parts) and it had failed completely and closed after only a few performances. But in London, given, as I thought, a much inferior production, with Isobel Elsom and Matheson Lang as the other two stars, the play achieved a considerable run. But Farquharson and Lang were reputed not to get on well together and I seemed to be aware of their disharmony, so that their performances, though individually effective enough, failed to satisfy me. Still, Farquharson was always much in demand for highly coloured characters, and Lewis Casson and Sybil Thorndike engaged him to play Iachimo in their production of *Cymbeline* and also Count Cenci in Shelley's tragedy, which they were adventurous enough to present for special matinées.

In the early Thirties he appeared as Cardinal Wolsey, with Flora Robson as Queen Katharine and Charles Laughton as Henry the Eighth, under Tyrone Guthrie's direction, at Sadler's Wells and the Old Vic. In 1958, when I was acting the part of Wolsey myself at the Old Vic (with Edith Evans as Katharine and Harry Andrews as the King) I was walking along the Kings Road, Chelsea, one fine morning when I suddenly saw Farquharson, at the age of eighty, perilously riding a bicycle among the heavy traffic. I waved to him rather timidly and was greatly surprised when he lightly vaulted off the bicycle and wheeled it on to the pavement. "How are you J-J-Jack?" he cried (no one had called me Jack since I first went on the stage in 1921). "All right," I answered, rather self-consciously. "You know I'm trying to play your part in *Henry the Eighth*." "Oh yes," he said, "I know. We both made the s-s-same mistake. We ought to have padded ourselves and made ourselves look enormously f-f-fat. When I played it the whole production was geared to show off s-s-some film actor or other, and when I came on, the director lowered all the lights and wheeled an enormous s-s-s-sideboard on to the stage which extinguished me entirely." So saying he guided his bicycle off the pavement, sprang into the saddle, and, in his green tweed suit and brown boots, disappeared among the tangle of cars and buses and was lost to me for ever.

9

TWO EXQUISITE COMEDIENNES

DAME MARIE TEMPEST AND YVONNE ARNAUD

During the Twenties and Thirties there were perhaps half a dozen famous names prominently displayed in lights over the entrances of the theatres, though the plays might often prove to be of considerably less distinction than the players who adorned them. The fashionable little comedies of those days would often begin at half-past eight or a quarter to nine, and, with two intervals, enlivened by a small and scratchy orchestra sawing away in the recesses of a tiny pit covered with imitation palm-leaves, the final curtain would often fall well before eleven o'clock. But the public seldom seemed to resent such scanty fare, especially when the names of Marie Tempest or Yvonne Arnaud twinkled in lights above the title of the play.

Both actresses were short and a little plump, but they were fascinating performers and played with inimitable inventiveness and style. With a wink here, a nod there, a giggle or a pout, absurd displays of temper or tears among the teacups, an expressive use of a tiny handkerchief, they could provoke or stifle laughter, point a line or repair a moment or two of emotional stress. Experts in phrasing and timing (both were trained musicians) they would take the stage like Millamant, "sails spread, with a shoal of fools for tenders," the one with her short brisk steps and bristling with authority, the other bustling about with endearing liveliness and humour.

DAME MARIE TEMPEST

My first two meetings with Marie Tempest were somewhat intimidating occasions. At a smart lunch party at which I had been introduced to her for the first time, she suddenly announced that the strap which held her shoes had become undone and I was despatched to the host's bedroom to find a button-hook. Kneeling clumsily beneath the tablecloth I dug the implement fiercely into the curve of her instep and emerged covered with confusion. One afternoon, a few days later, as I was going round to see a member of her company, she suddenly appeared, veiled and cloaked, at the stage-door, impatient to get home for the evening rest which was such an important item in her inflexible routine. Hoping she might remember me, I crushed her tiny fingers brutally in what I hoped was a manly handshake, and thought I heard her mutter fiercely "Blast you!" (though such an expression from such august lips seemed wildly improbable) as she plunged into her waiting car and was driven away.

When she created the part of the actress Judith Bliss in Noël Coward's *Hay Fever* at the Ambassadors Theatre in 1925 she immediately regained the enormous popularity which was to continue during the rest of her career. Her prestige had been somewhat in eclipse after she returned to London in

Esmé Percy with his last dog, Skippo

I once spent a weekend with him in Paris, and we were both invited to lunch at the British Embassy. In the morning we went up to Montmartre to see some Waxworks which were shown there, and this kept us amused for a longer time than we realised. As we came out it suddenly began to pour with rain, and we took refuge in a rather squalid bar nearby, where I felt very ill at ease and conspicuously British in my dark suit. But within only a few minutes, Esmé had charmed everybody in the bistro with his fluent French and easy friendliness, and, almost before we realised it, two formidable local apaches had rushed out into the downpour and returned with a taxi to convey us punctually to our lunch party.

Marie Tempest, 1906

She could be very mischievous on the stage when she was bored or disapproving of the players she was acting with, though she capitulated if she was directly challenged by anyone who was not afraid of her. Margaret Rutherford had the courage to stand up to her in an early success she made, when Dame Marie attempted to distract the audience by deliberately drawing attention away from her in a comedy scene in which they were acting together.

At matinées she would sometimes tap the teacups with a spoon and mutter, nearly but not quite audibly, to the other actors, "Get on, get on. I want my tea."

When a young actress tried to upstage her in an important scene, Dame Marie had the legs of the young lady's chair screwed down to the floor of the stage and watched with a grim smile as she attempted to move it.

On the first night of *Dear Octopus* in London she was extremely nervous and I followed her across the back of the stage as she went to make an entrance, the white cloak overall which she always wore over her stage costume billowing round her, and her dresser holding up the hem. She always disobeyed the rule of no smoking and ashtrays were fixed to the back of the scenery for her. The stage manager opened the door by which she was to enter and Marie Tempest slipped off her overall, crushed out her cigarette in the ashtray and preceded by a cloud of smoke stepped onto the scene with arms outstretched, a demure picture of grandmotherly affection, to greet the stage family awaiting her.

Ronald Squire, Yvonne Arnaud, and Leslie Faber in
By Candle Light at the Prince of Wales Theatre, 1928

Squire and Yvonne Arnaud professed to dislike each other, though they were partners in so many successes. He would refer to her as "that Belgian bitch" (though not with any real malice), and she would say, "Ah, dear Ronnie, he is so lazy! He falls asleep on the stage while other people are talking, and one has to send him champagne to perk him up."

Faber told me that he learned his craft understudying established stars like Sir Charles Wyndham and Sir George Alexander, and acting in "curtain raisers." These were one act plays presented before the main attractions in the fashionable West End theatres of the period, to keep the cheap parts of the audience amused while the smart occupants of the stalls and boxes gradually strolled in from late dinners in time to see the stars appearing in the principal attraction.

Cedric Hardwicke and Gwen Ffrangcon-Davies in
The Barretts of Wimpole Street, at the Queen's Theatre, 1930

An impressive performance as the hateful incestuous Father. His manner in the part was very subtly sinister . . . He was splendid, too, as the miserly Dr. Haggett in *The Late Christopher Bean* which he acted for many months at the St. James's in London, with Edith Evans in the part of the maidservant, played in New York by Pauline Lord.

1922 from a world tour and, failing for several seasons to find a suitable vehicle for her talents, she was even forced to play some secondary parts. But she took these reverses in her stride and was soon rewarded with the play she needed. The young playgoers who saw her in *Hay Fever* for the first time marvelled at her grace and composure, her wit and technical skill, while her old admirers continued to praise her beautiful diction and phrasing (she had been trained as a singer by Garcia, and triumphed as a star in light opera during her early years), and to delight in the unfailing distinction with which she walked the stage or sat erect, with her tiny elegantly shod feet crossed in front of her, wearing beautifully cut clothes and (as Noël Coward used to say) one of her crisp little hats.

She was in Edwardian travelling dress when I saw her first, acting in a revival of *Alice Sit by the Fire*—a sentimental Barrie play which hardly suited her better than it had suited Ellen Terry, for whom it was originally written—and on her first entrance she appeared in a hat which seemed to consist of an entire pheasant, with the beak standing guard above her turned-up nose. The audience applauded vigorously, and she came forward from the open doorway and smiled and bowed her acknowledgements to left and right before beginning her performance. This was the practice of all the great stars of that period—Mrs. Patrick Campbell, Irene Vanbrugh, Marion Terry, Julia Neilson—though today we should certainly think such behaviour very odd. On the first night of one of Milne's light comedies the director had even thoughtfully provided a large tray (set out on a sideboard with several vases of artificial flowers) for Irene Vanbrugh to carry round the stage, putting them down on various tables, in order to cover the tremendous applause which greeted her first entrance.

Marie Tempest was very fond of clothes, and wore them to

perfection. The short skirts of the Twenties suited her extremely well, and she used to wear pearl stud earrings, one black and one pink, if I remember rightly, and her hair was discreetly tinted to reddish gold. She was meticulous in the care of her stage dresses, always wore a light white cloak over her costume in passing from her dressing-room to the stage, and insisted that all the other ladies in the cast should do the same. Once made up and dressed, she never sat down in her dressing-room but stood on a white drugget, and so her dresses were always fresh and seldom had to be replaced during a long run. It was said that the new shoes ordered to go with each dress were sent straight to her own house, and she would bring old ones to wear in the play that were more comfortable. On one occasion a rather emotional young actress, who had been deservedly chidden for unpunctuality and carelessness during a performance, flung herself at Marie Tempest's feet to beg her pardon, but Dame Marie cut her short with a toss of her head and the brusque command, "Get up! Get up! Have you no respect for your management's clothes?"

She was a martinet, severe and didactic even to her friends, and a demon of discipline in the theatre. But her bark was worse than her bite. Her marriage to Graham Browne was an ideal partnership, and they had already lived devotedly together for many years before they were able to be married. Browne was a good actor—better sometimes than he was given credit for, as he always stood back to give the limelight to his wife—and a charming, modest man. He died in 1937 during the run of a play entitled *Retreat from Folly* in which they were, as usual, acting together. On the morning of the funeral Marie Tempest ordered her car and came downstairs in a summer frock, having first made sure that all the flowers and wreaths which filled the hall should be cleared away. She

spent the morning at the Queen's Theatre rehearsing with her
husband's understudy and appeared as usual at the evening
performance, disregarding the inevitable criticisms of those
who were unkind enough to accuse her of indifference and
thought she should have closed the theatre.

She never appeared in the classics, though Sheridan and
Congreve would surely have suited her stylishness to perfection. My father always compared her favourably with Réjane
and Mrs. Kendal (both of whom he admired enormously,
though I never saw either of them on the stage myself) but
both of these actresses had been equally accomplished mis-
tresses of pathos as well as comedy. Much as I revelled in
Marie Tempest's comic gifts, I always found her less convincing in the few dramatic scenes I saw her play. However, those
who were lucky enough to remember a stage version of *Vanity
Fair,* in which she made a big dramatic success as Becky Sharp,
maintained that it was the fault of the playwrights that she was
not provided with better opportunities to show the more
serious possibilities of which she was capable. Her acting in
two fine death scenes, both in the Edna Ferber-George S.
Kaufman *Theatre Royal* (the British title for *The Royal
Family*), in which she appeared with Madge Titheradge and
Laurence Olivier, and in *Little Catherine,* a Russian melodrama
from the French of Alfred Savoir which ran for a very few
weeks and was only remembered for her fine performance in
it, showed her to great advantage in contrast to her usual run
of frivolous parts. But in *The First Mrs. Fraser,* by St. John
Ervine, I overheard a rival actress sitting near me murmuring
(with some fairness), "Oh, I can't be very pleased with Mary
for that," as the curtain fell on an emotional scene.

Her Stage Jubilee took place at Drury Lane Theatre in
1937, and I had the honour of being chosen to recite some
verses introducing a great pageant of players marshalled by

Tyrone Guthrie in her honour. Royalty was in a box, and Marie Tempest was carried on in a big gold chair, wearing a soft pink chiffon dress which floated round her as she made her faltering (but expert) little speech of thanks, curtsying first to the King and Queen and then to the audience, with her usual consummate grace. Then, after the curtain had finally fallen, she turned and bowed to us all, and, frail, tiny, but still immensely dignified, walked away to her dressing-room.

She continued acting for five years more with undiminished energy, both in London and on tour. She moved to a new flat and decorated her rooms, continued to buy bibelots, dinner services, presents, and to regulate her household with minute attention. From her dressing-room she would send for members of her company and lecture them individually, questioning them about their health, their love-affairs, and their behaviour generally, in private life as well as on the stage, and giving practical orders and advice. She was interested in every detail—in their diets, doctors, and dentists and the workings of their insides as well as in their acting.

I was with her when she created her last new role, Dora Randolph, the grandmother in Dodie Smith's *Dear Octopus,* produced at the Queen's Theatre on the eve of Munich. She behaved impeccably at rehearsals, though we were all a little afraid of her at first, but the young director, Glen Byam Shaw, handled her with perfect tact, and she listened to him obediently. She had some difficulty in learning her lines, and we were convinced that, except for her own part, she had never even read the play. "Are those some of my children?" she would inquire doubtfully, as another of the large assembly of characters came forward to greet her. One day she sent us all away while she took a lesson to learn "The Kerry Dances," two verses of which she was to sing in the nursery scene. When we returned some hours later she had mastered it with apparent ease, and sang it enchantingly at the cottage piano, her voice still sweet and true. In the last act I liked to watch her in the scene when she was folding napkins for a dinner party in the shape of water-lilies. She was supposed to have drunk a cocktail and was a little tipsy, throwing one of the napkins into the air and catching it just in time with a wicked chuckle.

We became great friends during the run. I would be invited every evening to go to her dressing-room during one of my waits. There, with the white drugget on the floor and the patience cards laid out (she always played patience every night when she arrived at the theatre) I would be given French bread and butter and a cup of coffee, served by her dresser-companion with impressive ceremony.

When we were in Newcastle to try out the play, Marie Tempest insisted on coming down every morning in the hotel, always beautifully dressed. Sometimes she wore a big shady straw hat with a gardenia decorating the brim, and she always turned back her white gloves over the wrists as she ate her lunch. Sometimes we would go for a short drive together before her afternoon rest, and it was amusing to watch her choosing a cock-lobster ("not a hen," she stipulated firmly) after she had climbed in her high heels over a steep step into the little whitewashed cottage where the woman who was selling the lobsters had her shop. The creatures were scuttling about all over the stone floor, but Marie Tempest went on calmly chattering to her and seemed to understand what she was saying, despite her very thick Northumbrian accent.

When the war broke out, *Dear Octopus* closed in London. Her Regent's Park flat was bombed, and she moved for a few weeks to Great Fosters, the hotel near Windsor, where I also happened to be staying for a few nights while I was making a film at Teddington. Here I would encounter her among the other residents, walking impatiently to and fro in the Great Hall during an air raid, impeccable as ever in a suit of blue slacks, and as a particularly loud explosion shook the walls I heard her remark to her companion, *"Quelle vie de dog!"* (A rival actress was once heard to remark, "Do you think Mary speaks what they call working French?")

My contract in *Dear Octopus* had expired and I left the play which had resumed its run after the blitz, but she continued acting in it for many months. Not long afterwards she was taken ill. I went to call on her with books and flowers, but after ten minutes' nervous conversation she caught me surreptitiously looking at my watch. "It was sweet of you to come, my dear," she said drily, "but you think me rather an old bore really, don't you?" I felt deeply ashamed, for I loved and admired her very much. But a few days later, in October 1942, she was dead.

YVONNE ARNAUD

Yvonne Arnaud, like Marie Tempest, was a brilliant musician. She had been something of a prodigy as a child pianist, playing in public with big orchestras abroad. She then achieved great success on the stage in London, where she sang and danced in *The Girl in the Taxi*. This I never saw, but I well remember the coloured poster which advertised it—a man and a girl getting into a cab from opposite sides, "Mine I think! Mine I believe!" "Ours I hope!" She was delightful as Mrs. Pepys in James Bernard Fagan's play, *And So to Bed,* after she had been leading lady in the splendid "Aldwych farces" with Ralph Lynn, Tom Walls, and Mary Brough. In the first of these, *Tons of Money,* she scored with a wonderfully funny gag-line at every crisis, "Aubrey, I've got an idea," delivered in her inimitable broken English. In *By Candle Light,* an adaptation from the Viennese, she was a perfect foil for Leslie Faber and Ronald Squire, but this success was sadly interrupted by Faber's sudden and untimely death.

When I first acted in New York, in 1928 at the Majestic, she was playing at the theatre next door, the Shubert, with the English company of *And So to Bed,* and Emlyn Williams, then a young man of twenty-two, was in the cast. Emlyn and I would go off to speakeasies (knocking at the gratings of little doors and fearing we should be blinded by bathtub gin) and Yvonne Arnaud was enchantingly kind to me whenever I was lucky enough to meet her.

Fifteen years later, during the Second War, when she had starred in a number of very slight comedies and carried most of them to success on her supremely capable shoulders, I remembered her performance as Mrs. Pepys, and persuaded her to appear as Mrs. Frail in a revival that I was planning of Congreve's *Love for Love.* There was some trouble over her costumes, for she could not wear the correctly tight corsets of the period as she had a weak chest and caught bronchitis and bad colds very easily. But she compromised with bones sewn into her bodices, and when, at the dress parade, she stepped on to the stage at the Opera House, Manchester (where we opened the play), spreading her fan and smoothing out her ample skirts, and remarked with a sly wink, "Not so bad, do you think, for an old girl!" I was her devoted slave.

She would not sleep in London during air raids but would send her dresser out to shop for her, rushing off to Waterloo as soon as the play was over laden with bags and parcels, and riding triumphantly in the guards van of a train to reach her country house, coaxing smiles and friendly help from everyone on the way.

When she was ill for several weeks and unable to appear, the play suffered dreadfully without her. We all loved the way she

shared our scenes with us, and the skill she could use to cover
weaknesses if she was acting with a less accomplished per-
former than herself.

Her technique was as unfailing as her instinct. One might
have supposed that the elaborate verbiage of Congreve would
have proved something of a problem for her, with her French
accent, after a lifetime of speaking modern colloquial dialogue, but she used her breathing and timing as cunningly as
ever and rose to the challenge like a bird. She was the only
leading actress I have ever known who looked forward to a
first night with happy anticipation and really seemed to enjoy
every single moment of it. She should of course have played in
some of the Molière comedies and the farces of Feydeau. Best
of all, what fun it would have been if one had ever been able to
see her acting in a play with Marie Tempest!

10

THREE GREAT CHARACTER ACTORS

LESLIE FABER, SIR CEDRIC HARDWICKE, CHARLES LAUGHTON

LESLIE FABER

Leslie Faber was a tall, distinguished-looking man with pale blue eyes and a long upper lip. His fair hair, worn rather long and streaked with grey when I knew him, was brushed in wings round either side of his head. His clothes were dark and conventional. Only his hats, worn at a jaunty angle, had curly brims* and betrayed the actor. He somewhat resembled the well-known portraits of George Washington, as the American critics were quick to notice when he went to act in New York. He was of Danish extraction, and a photograph of him still hangs in the Theatre Museum at the Fredericksborg Castle in Copenhagen. He was the first West End star to take notice of

---

* Though not as curly as the hats worn by Allan Aynesworth, which were always strikingly individual.

me and encourage my early efforts as an actor, and apart from
that I was to grow deeply fond of him as a friend.

He was extremely successful in disguising himself and evolv-
ing clever make-ups. As a mysterious Count in a play called
In the Night he peered from underneath a large top hat and
was enveloped in a huge overcoat with a fur collar. As the
Scottish police doctor (who turned out to be the criminal when
they finally solved the mystery) in Edgar Wallace's *The Ringer,*
he had a square bowler, a red nose, baggy trousers and shabby
boots, and sucked endless cigarettes, holding them, between
puffs, in curled mittened fingers. But it was in *Jane Clegg,* a
gloomy kitchen-sink drama by St. John Ervine, that his acting
first made a great impression on me, though I remember little
of the play itself. His part was that of a drunken idle husband,
nagging and bullying his long-suffering wife (Sybil Thorndike) and his crotchety old mother-in-law (Clare Greet, a fine
old actress who had created Shaw's Rummy Mitchens in
Major Barbara and the charwoman in *Outward Bound*). But
he was splendid too in straight parts, and I greatly admired
his performances in various melodramas—*Havoc, The Outsider, White Cargo, The Sign on the Door,* and Maugham's
The Letter, in all of which he acted with power, sensitivity,
and taste. But his greatest success proved ironically to be his
last. He went into management with Ronald Squire, and they
presented together a delightful comedy, *By Candle Light,* in
which Leslie Faber as the Baron and Squire as his valet acted
the two leading parts, with Yvonne Arnaud, at her enchanting
best, as a *soubrette* maid. But Faber was working too hard,
filming during the day as well as acting in the theatre every
night, and he caught pneumonia after a weekend cruise on a
boat he had just bought to celebrate the success of the play,
and died after only a short illness.

He had always longed to succeed in romantic parts, but

there was something austere in his personality which stood in his way. He could convey sensuality but not great warmth. His natural hauteur must have been effective when he played Jason to Sybil Thorndike's Medea, but apparently he failed when he played Shakespeare's Richard the Second for some special Sunday night performance. He must have invited me to watch a rehearsal, for I have a vivid recollection of him sitting in a big chair, dressed in a dark business suit, with a Homburg hat tilted over one eye for a crown, and an incongruous sceptre held in the crook of his arm, but I never saw him play the part, though he told me afterwards that he had failed to please himself in it. I found in him, as in many fine actors, a strange mixture of vanity, confidence, and self-dissatisfaction. He could be extremely generous, and was always enchantingly kind both to me and my brother Val (who was understudying and walking-on in *The Ringer* when he first met him) but he could also be narrow-minded, bitter and suspicious, and I think he felt he had never achieved the position to which his talents should have entitled him.

He wore period costume with ease, and was a fine Macduff in a very bad production of *Macbeth* in which the American star, James Hackett, appeared with Mrs. Patrick Campbell. He would, I am sure, have been an ideal Joseph Surface, but I do not think he ever played the part. He was also a most talented director, and I was lucky enough to work under him on two occasions for special performances in the early Twenties. I was already secretly cherishing an ambition to direct a play myself, and watched with admiration the way in which Faber handled the authors and players under his control, making tactful but important adjustments in the texts, and illuminating the action by the way in which he arranged the entrances and exits and the disposition of the characters.

In the second of these Sunday productions he acted the

leading part himself as well as directing the play, a romantic costume melodrama called *Huntersmoon* (adapted I think from the Danish) in which my second cousin, Phyllis Neilson-Terry, who had given me my first professional engagement in 1921, played the heroine, and I was cast as her cowardly husband. Faber's part was a kind of Sydney Carton character, secretly in love with the heroine for whom he sacrificed his life in the last act. He was modest enough to ask me what I thought of his performance, and I ventured to say that I thought he should take the stage more boldly and sweep the audience off their feet in the manner of my great-uncle Fred Terry, Phyllis's father. But he smiled sadly and said he only wished he could act like that.

In 1928 he went, with Lyn Harding and Madge Titheradge, to New York, to appear for Gilbert Miller in a German play, *The Patriot,* translated and adapted by Ashley Dukes. A young actor playing the Tsarevitch proved inadequate and Faber cabled suggesting me as a substitute. I sailed immediately and arrived in time for the dress-rehearsal, having learnt my short but effective part on board ship. But New York would have none of the play and we sadly returned to London after only ten days' run.

In the following year, Faber invited me to go with him to see the English production of the same play, renamed *Such Men Are Dangerous,* with Matheson Lang in the leading part. We both felt the later version to be inferior to the one in which we had appeared in America, but Lang was a great favourite in London, and achieved considerable personal success. He was a fine actor too, less subtle, to my mind, than Leslie, but with greater sex-appeal.

When Faber died, the obituary notices gave a long list of his successful appearances and praised his fine career, but I al-

ways felt that his somewhat cynical manner covered an unhappy personal life and a deep sense of disappointment even
with the work he loved so well.

SIR CEDRIC HARDWICKE

Cedric Hardwicke was not unlike Faber in some respects—the
same long upper lip and slightly sardonic reserve. He was somewhat forbidding in straight parts, but could be very endearing
when he was able to disguise his appearance and create odd
characters quite unlike himself. He was superb as Churdles Ash
in *The Farmer's Wife* and in *Yellow Sands,* two Eden Phil-
potts comedies in which he scored enormous personal successes, and he was always good in Shaw—as the He-Ancient in
Back to Methusalah, as Caesar (with Gwen Ffrangcon-Davies
as Cleopatra), as Shotover in *Heartbreak House* and Magnus
in *The Apple Cart* with Edith Evans. He was the Gravedigger
in the first modern-dress Shakespearean production, with Colin
Keith-Johnston as the Prince (it was christened "Hamlet in
Plus Fours"), and of course I was greatly impressed by his
performance as the hateful incestuous Father in *The Barretts
of Wimpole Street,* again opposite Gwen Ffrangcon-Davies.
His manner in this part was very subtly sinister, the mouth
drawn down at the edges in a hypocritical sneer, with pious
looks to Heaven as he made Henrietta swear on the Bible or
forced Elizabeth to drink the mug of porter, and the pouting
of his sensual lips as he ordered the dog to be destroyed.*

His voice was rather dry and thick, but he used it with admirable effect in dialect and light comedy, though I think he

---

*I attempted the same role in a film remake of the play in 1958, and
felt I was able to do little justice to the part.

did not have the range for tragic parts. A season with the Old
Vic Company at the New Theatre, when he played Gaev to
Edith Evans's Madame Ranevsky in *The Cherry Orchard,* and
also Sir Toby Belch, with great success, was spoilt for him by an
ill-fated production in which he was persuaded to appear as
Faustus in Marlowe's tragedy. He had a long and distinguished
career in films, both in England and California, but in his last
years he seemed to lose heart and to break little fresh ground
either in the cinema or the theatre.

We worked together only once, in Laurence Olivier's film
of *Richard the Third,* and Ralph Richardson, one of his oldest
and dearest friends, was also in the cast as Buckingham. Cedric
Hardwicke seemed terribly depressed during our days together in the studio, and we all tried to cheer him up. "I'm
too old for this Shakespeare business," he would say. I asked
him what he was planning to do next, "Oh," he said, "I have
to go back to California to play Moses in *The Ten Commandments* and Louis the Eleventh in a musical of *If I Were King.*"
"Good parts?" I asked. "Oh Heaven knows," said Hardwicke
gloomily, "my agent reads the scripts for me. I would never
agree to do them if I had to choose them for myself."

In his last success in the theatre he played, in New York, a
Japanese gentleman in a light comedy, *A Majority of One,*
starring with a well-known Jewish comedienne, Gertrude
Berg. I was acting at a theatre nearby in *Much Ado About
Nothing* with Margaret Leighton, and we would both dine
with Cedric between performances on matinée days at Sardi's,
where he seemed happy to be with us and chattered delightfully on all sorts of topics. But we both felt that he was lonely
and only the shadow of his former self. Like Faber, he had
unhappy marriages and lost most of the money he had made
in his most successful years. He spent his last months living
alone in a hotel and died quite soon afterwards. He always

seemed to be vaguely surprised at having received his knight-hood and the high esteem in which he was held in his profession. I always loved Hardwicke's own story of being knighted by George the Fifth, who was deaf, and the King, prompted by a whisper from his equerry, saying, "Rise, Sir Samuel Pickwick." I should have liked to have known him better and perhaps been able to show him more sympathy and encouragement at a time when he must have needed them so badly.

CHARLES LAUGHTON

Cedric Hardwicke and Leslie Faber were both, I think, well aware of their physical and vocal limitations. Charles Laughton, who, despite a brilliantly versatile career, was more successful (first in the theatre and afterwards on the screen) than either of the other two, never achieved a real triumph in the parts he most longed to play. At the Old Vic he acted Macbeth with little success, insisted on choosing the part of Prospero rather than Caliban, in which he should have been superb, and never tackled Falstaff, a character for which in many ways he would surely have been ideally suited. Although he triumphed in Korda's film, *The Private Life of Henry the Eighth,* he made no great impact when he appeared as Shakespeare's Henry at Sadler's Wells at the Vic under Tyrone Guthrie, though his magnificent Angelo in *Measure for Measure,* and his Lopahin in *The Cherry Orchard* during the same season, were unforgettably fine performances. His film creation of Captain Bligh in *Mutiny on the Bounty* was to bring him world-wide recognition,* but his return to the theatre was less successful

---

* He also played Moulton-Barrett in *The Barretts of Wimpole Street* with great success in the first film version of the play with Norma Shearer and Fredric March.

when, after a long absence, he appeared in Brecht's *Galileo* and as Undershaft in Shaw's *Major Barbara* (under Orson Welles's direction) in New York, and came back to appear at Stratford as Bottom and King Lear, and in London in a play called *The Party,* by Jane Arden when he was theatrical god-father to the young Albert Finney. He had become something of a legend in California, where he trained pupils, gave read-ings from the Bible and the classics, and took part in a famous reading of the "Don Juan in Hell" scene from Shaw's *Man and Superman* with Cedric Hardwicke, Charles Boyer, and Agnes Moorehead. He was already ill before he returned to Los Angeles, where he died not long afterwards—in 1962.

In the early Twenties, when he suddenly burst on London, his talent and versatility had taken the town by storm. He ar-rived from Yorkshire with a scholarship to the R.A.D.A., where Alice Gachet, a very perceptive teacher, coached him in some scenes in French, and at once became convinced of his great potential talent. Soon afterwards he was engaged for a part in Molnar's *Liliom* with Fay Compton, but the play failed completely. (It was the second version to be done in London, and equally unsuccessful on both occasions, though in New York the Theatre Guild had one of its first successes with it, starring Joseph Schildkraut and Eva Le Gallienne, and later the musical version *Carousel* was to be enormously popular.) At the Duke of York's Theatre in London it was directed by Komisarjevsky, who, with his usual perversity, undertook the production, although he thoroughly disapproved of the cast-ing of Fay Compton and Ivor Novello in leading parts. Charles Laughton, however, in a minor role (the Apache friend of the hero) scored an immediate personal triumph, and shortly afterwards was to be seen, again under Komisarjevsky's direction, at the Barnes Theatre, as Solyony, the sinister officer with the scent-bottle in *The Three Sisters,* and as Epihodov in

The Cherry Orchard. He was soon in demand in the West End where he acted in a series of plays of many different kinds. He appeared as the beaming detective Poirot in Agatha Christie's *Alibi,* and gave a sensational melodramatic performance as a Chicago gangster (derived from Al Capone) in Edgar Wallace's *On the Spot,* and a fascinating study of a seedy murderer in *Payment Deferred* by Jeffrey Dell from the novel by E. M. Forster which he later repeated on the screen.

Laughton, as I knew him in those early days, was an amiable mixture of boyish gaiety, moodiness, and charm. When he was first married to Elsa Lanchester they had a tree-house in the country, where they used to spend weekends, and in London they lived in a charming flat in Gordon Square. I remember going to a party there. The big sitting-room had double doors, decorated with paintings of animals by the designer John Armstrong. Round the walls were low open bookshelves, lit from underneath, while on the glass shelves which ran along the top of them were specimen vases, filled with sprigs of blossom and single branches of foliage, which they had brought back from the country and arranged with exquisite taste.

I never knew Laughton very well. His acting did not rely on mimicry and I was greatly struck with the way in which, in spite of his own extraordinary individuality, he always seemed able to sink himself completely in a new part and find new colours and different ranges of voice for the characters he played. His old senator with the Southern accent in the film *Advise and Consent,* made very late in his career, was marvellously detailed and convincing.

His personality was as flexible as his appearance. He could be boyishly attractive or decadently sinister, with a menacing quality that might have made him a fine interpreter of Pinter. When he was cast as Worthing in *The Importance of Being*

Earnest in his Old Vic season, Tyrone Guthrie thought him so unpleasant that he took the part away from him and persuaded him to play Dr. Chasuble, the oily rector, instead. But I always admired his courage in revealing the sensual side of his nature with such honesty and power. In the part of Angelo he trod the stage like an evil bat, with the billowing silk sleeves of his black gown flapping round him as he prowled up and down the stage, and he had immense drive, with a strong vein of poetic imagination which gave his performances colour and excitement. One might say, perhaps, that whereas Faber and Hardwicke were highly skilled dyed-in-the-wool professionals, Laughton was an inspired amateur. The first two men were perfectionists, calculating their acting to a nicety, and both struck me as being basically modest men, dry, witty, cynical. Laughton was more of an exhibitionist. His monsters were vicious with a kind of childlike *naïveté* fascinating in its contradictions. In *Macbeth* he made a sensation only in the Banquet Scene when confronted with the Ghost of Banquo, while in *King Lear* his scene on Dover Cliff made the greatest impression. He could not find and sustain the progression necessary to achieve either of these great parts to the full. How often stage and screen, dividing the loyalties of talented actors, have played havoc with their sense of direction and crippled their potentialities in consequence.

11

A BRILLIANT LEADING LADY

GERTRUDE LAWRENCE

Theatre audiences (and women especially), are apt to waste a great deal of time speculating on the ages of the actresses they have come to see. At the opening of a new revue at Manchester, for instance, I once sat behind two ladies who wrangled over the possible ages of Beatrice Lillie and Madge Elliott all through the interval, as well as whispering continually during the performance on the same absorbing topic. But Gertrude Lawrence was such a mercurial creature that the question of her age never occurred to one when she was acting, and when she died at the peak of her career in September 1952, her public and fellow players on both sides of the Atlantic were equally shocked, and the lights outside the theatres both on Broadway and in London were lowered to pay tribute to her memory.

I was never lucky enough to act with her, but once when we were both appearing in New York (she with Noël Cow-

ard in *Tonight at 8:30* and I in *Hamlet*), we were asked to
take part in a great Midnight Charity Ball at the Astor Hotel.
Gertrude Lawrence, as "Day," was led into the ballroom on a
large white horse. It was a very broad-beamed animal and she
gave one look at it and remarked, "A few inches wider and
I shan't be able to make the matinée tomorrow." As "Night,"
I bestrode an equally imposing black steed. Our costumes had
been specially designed by James Reynolds, a distinguished
theatre-artist of the day, and I wore a helmet with long
plumes and imposing-looking boots, though I only discovered at the last moment that they had thin paper soles, making it very difficult for me to mount and dismount with rea-
sonable dignity. We were conducted on horseback all round
the room, glancing somewhat apprehensively at the slippery
floor, and were greeted with polite applause. Our mounts
were then led away, and we took our places on two thrones
facing each other, where we sat gazing at the back of Gypsy
Rose Lee as she performed an elegant strip-tease, while the
Honourable Thelma Furness, as the "Sun," wearing a golden
crown with large spiky rays attached to it, surveyed the scene
from above us on another throne. Once the cermony was
over, however, we were completely forgotten by everyone,
and we found ourselves standing rather forlornly together at
the bar, drinking gin and tonics with our dressers and glad to
slip away immediately afterwards.

Noël Coward has always said that Gertrude Lawrence's instinct was so incredibly quick and true that she ought to be
sent home after the first reading of a new play and not be allowed to reappear until the first performance. She was always
full of mischief, and incredibly versatile and unpredictable,
even in private life. She was declared bankrupt while she was
trying out a play in Manchester, and her financial affairs were
usually in disorder, but this did not deter her from gaily or-

Cronin Wilson, Charles Laughton, and Ben Weldon in *On the Spot*
at Wyndham's Theatre, 1930

His rich voice could suddenly rise to a coldblooded sneering whiplash that chilled
one's blood, and after his success as Captain Bligh, he became a popular favourite
for imitation among nightclub mimics But he could also be bland and creamily
charming, with a babyish smile and an endearing frankness of expression. He made
one of his first Hollywood successes in the part of a gentleman's gentleman in the
film *Ruggles of Red Gap* who in one scene recited Lincoln's Gettysburg Address,
with enormous success, in impeccable English accents.

Noël Coward and Gertrude Lawrence in *Private Lives*
at the Phoenix Theatre, 1930

One of Gertrude Lawrence's last appearances in London was in a play called *September Tide* by Daphne du Maurier. The dowager Queen Mary, an ardent theatregoer, was in a box one evening and, as was her custom, sent for the principal players to be presented to her during an interval period.

"I am enjoying the performance very much," she remarked, then added somewhat severely, "but I'm afraid I am finding it rather difficult to hear." "Ah," said Gertrude Lawrence brightly, turning to the juvenile couple who played the young people, "we must all take care to speak up then, mustn't we?" Queen Mary raised her lorgnette and remarked firmly, "No, Miss Lawrence, *You* must."

Lady Cunard, *c.* 1937

An American and patroness of the arts, whose two most intimate friends were George Moore, the writer, and Sir Thomas Beecham, the eminent conductor.

dering her flat to be redecorated or commissioning a new Rolls-Royce to be specially built for her, though quite forgetting to pay some small outstanding laundry bill.

She had beautiful jewels and was excessively generous. Edward Molyneux had given her *carte blanche* on condition that he provided her with her entire wardrobe, yet she could not resist sneaking off and buying dresses from other houses. She was apt to assume a different role on different days—the great Star, the Mother figure, the Cockney guttersnipe (she was Eliza Doolittle in Shaw's play in New York, and I would have given much to have seen her play it) or the industrious, approachable actress—all presented with equal skill and charm.

Her greatest fault (according to Coward who had many rows with her about it) was to embroider her performance after a few weeks with improvisations and funny business which sometimes spoiled the clean line of her otherwise brilliant readings. She had a seemingly effortless technique. Her features were irregular, with a strange blob of a nose, but she had beautiful eyes and hands, wore clothes like a dream, and danced with exquisite grace. Although her voice was never very good (she wobbled if she had to sustain a high note and was frequently out of tune) she had learned to use it with beguiling charm.

In "Fallen Babies," a sketch in Charlot's Revue (produced at the same time as Coward's play *Fallen Angels*) she and Beatrice Lillie were wheeled on to the stage in a huge double pram, with large rubber teats in their mouths. I think they drank cocktails too and chattered together in racy terms. I have two other favourite memories of her in Coward's first revue *London Calling!*—one a monologue (which she played sitting up in a large bed, talking on the telephone to various friends in different voices) in which she was supposed to be a chorus-girl called Poppy Baker—the other, "Parisian Pierrot," a song which she made nostalgically romantic, lying on a sofa of coloured cushions wearing black pyjamas. In another revue she was a slinky Chinese girl singing "Limehouse Blues." She could be fashionable, pathetic, or broadly comic in successive scenes, changing from one mood to another without the slightest appearance of effort. Her forgetful hostess in Coward's *Hands Across the Sea* was hilariously funny, but she was equally brilliant half-an-hour later as the slatternly wife in *Fumed Oak,* eating a disgusting-looking bloater and picking the fish bones from between her teeth.

It was in revue and musical comedy that she had her greatest triumphs, though she also carried some rather indifferent straight comedies to success, and acted once in a serious drama of John Van Druten's *Behold, We Live,* in which she starred with Gerald du Maurier. She appeared in a number of films (*Rembrandt* with Charles Laughton was one of them) but she was, I imagine, not easy to photograph and the medium did not greatly suit her. I always wondered whether she might not have been fascinating as Lady Teazle or as Beatrice, but she never ventured further than Shaw in the classic field. I once spent an afternoon trying to persuade her to play Sophie Fullgarney in a revival of Pinero's *The Gay Lord Quex* but though she seemed interested I do not think she ever found time to read the play. But I am happy to think I saw her in *The King and I* in New York only a few months before her death, waltzing enchantingly round the stage with Yul Brynner in her billowing white satin crinoline. She was a fascinating enigmatic creature, and the gramophone records she left behind, especially the famous scene with Coward in *Private Lives* and another in which she sings some of her best songs, remain to evoke something of her personality for the present generation as well as for those of us who had the joy of seeing her on the stage.

12

TWO FORCEFUL ACTORS

ROBERT LORAINE AND CLAUDE RAINS

ROBERT LORAINE

Loraine was a powerful, expressive actor, broad-shouldered and possessed of a noble presence and a deep resonant voice. I thought his Cyrano perfection, and was greatly moved by his performance of Strindberg's *The Father* at the Everyman Theatre in the Twenties. I had also seen him as the young Australian soldier in Barrie's *Mary Rose* with Fay Compton at the Haymarket, and as Mirabell, to the definitive Millamant of Edith Evans, in *The Way of the World* when Nigel Playfair presented it at the Lyric, Hammersmith, but thought him a little heavy-handed for young romantic parts.

Shaw, who had saved him from drowning once when they were on a bathing expedition together, was always fond of him, and he was a splendid Bluntschli in *Arms and The Man* (in a revival charmingly designed by Hugo Rumbold) and had achieved great success as John Tanner in *Man and Super-man* both in England and America. I gather from various hints in letters that Shaw would have liked him to create the part of Higgins in the first production of *Pygmalion,* but that Mrs. Campbell firmly put her foot down. From my own slight personal experience of his behaviour and a considerable knowledge of her, I can well imagine that they would have been uneasy partners.

In 1927 I was asked to appear as Cassio to Loraine's Othello, for a Sunday night and Monday matinée, by the Fellowship of Players, with Ernest Thesiger as Roderigo, Ion Swinley as Iago, Gertrude Elliott (Lady Forbes-Robertson, Sir Johnston's widow) as Emilia, and Elissa Landi as Desdemona. Nobody was paid, of course, but actors and actresses would gladly play for the Sunday Societies in those days as a change from long runs, or in the hope of strengthening their technique and reputations if they were out of work.

James Whale (who directed the original *Journey's End* for the Stage Society and was to win fame as a film director in Hollywood not long afterwards) was in charge of the rehearsals. He was an old friend of mine from my days in J. B. Fagan's repertory theatre at Oxford. Every morning we would begin to rehearse without Othello, but some twenty minutes later Loraine, in a mackintosh and bowler hat, would breeze into the theatre and, regardless of us all, proceed to deliver the speech to the Senate from the centre of the stage, forcing our little group to abandon our efforts and huddle bashfully in the wings.

He listened to no one, least of all to the director, but made an exception in the case of Lady Forbes-Robertson, for whose advice he would occasionally ask. She brought along her husband's prompt-book, and Loraine, finding the epilepsy scene had been cut by the great man in his production, decided immediately that he would not play it either. Elissa Landi tried to protest at his violence as he strangled her in the final scene, but he quickly silenced her with a pillow, remarking firmly, "You mind your own business, my dear young lady, and I'll mind mine."

At the dress-rehearsal he kept us all waiting for nearly an hour while he indulged in a violent tantrum over his wig and costume, and later sent strict instructions to us all to quit the stage after the first company curtain at the end of the play so that he might take a call alone. At the actual performance he shooed us off like chickens and drew himself up in his robes to acknowledge his reception. I could not help smiling, as I stood in the wings, to see that Swinley (always the most enchantingly modest of men both on and off the stage) had braved the lightning by refusing to budge, and as the curtain had already gone up, Loraine could only blink at him furiously and pretend that he was only too delighted to share the honours with him after all.

The temperament of Othello may have been partly to blame on this occasion for such autocratic behaviour, though I think he was always a man of violent feeling. Edith Evans, however, told me that she greatly enjoyed acting with him in *The Way of the World* (they were together in another play, *Tiger Cats,* a sensational melodrama of no great account), and said he had once given her an excellent piece of advice. Beside the little Hammersmith theatre was a narrow alley, and the ragamuffins of the neighbourhood, who had nothing better to do, would knock with sticks and boots on the iron shutter of the scene dock, rattling and banging while the performance was going on and ruining the concentration of the actors. Loraine, however, turned to Edith Evans and remarked, "If something in the theatre is troublesome, and can possibly be put right, it is perfectly legitimate to make a fuss. Otherwise you had best ignore it and get on with your work."

But he could hardly have been able to ignore the situation

when, on the first night of his revival of *Cyrano* in London, the stage-hands, resenting his rude treatment of them at the dress-rehearsals, deliberately omitted to fasten the cleats holding up the stage tree under which Cyrano has to sit in the final scene, and the poor actor was forced to hold up the sagging piece of scenery with his back and finish the play as best he could.

CLAUDE RAINS

He had been call boy at His Majesty's Theatre under Tree, but by the time I first met him in the Twenties he was already much in demand as a successful character actor. He lacked inches and wore lifts in his shoes to increase his height. Stocky but handsome, with broad shoulders and a mop of thick brown hair which he brushed over one eye, he wore beautifully cut double-breasted suits, starched shirts with pointed collars and big cuffs, and wide satin ties. He had piercing dark eyes and a beautiful throaty voice, though he had, like Marlene Dietrich, some trouble with the letter "R." Extremely attractive to women, he was divorced several times, and once appeared (as Falkland in *The Rivals*) with Beatrix Thomson, to whom he was then married, in a cast that included two of his former wives. Needless to say, all the girls in my class at the Royal Academy of Dramatic Art, where he was one of the best and most popular teachers, were hopelessly in love with him.

I found him enormously helpful and encouraging to work with and was always trying to copy him in my first years as an actor, until I decided to imitate Noël Coward instead. As I understudied them both at different times, I suppose this was only to be expected. Rains, as Dubedat in *The Doctor's Di-*

lemma, was just the romantic boyish figure that I hoped to be, whether in his blue painter's smock sketching the doctors, or in the death scene, when he was wheeled on to the stage wrapped in a purple dressing-jacket with a rug over his knees, and his hands, made-up very white, hanging down over the arms of his chair.

He acted another artist, a sculptor this time, dying of morphine addiction, in a melodrama *Daniel* adapted from the French of Louis Verneuil. The part had been originally written for Sarah Bernhardt, who was seen in it during her last season in London. Though her leg had been amputated and she was over seventy, she contrived to give a remarkable effect of youth, and even masculinity, as she lay dying on a studio couch covered with rugs.

In the English version, Rains was extremely effective (Edith Evans, playing a silly mother in a white wig, who was always taking pills in the first act, was also in the cast), and a year or two later I was actually engaged myself to appear in the same character in an adaptation of the story for the cinema. This was my first silent film, with Isobel Elsom, Henry Vibart, and Mary Rorke, and it was shot at Teddington in very hot weather. I tried to emote with suitable abandon, encouraged by music played "live" on a violin and piano in the film studio and a director who urged me on to absurdly melodramatic heights. In 1921 Nigel Playfair engaged me for my first London appearance in *The Insect Play* by the brothers Capek. He was to direct it at the Regent Theatre, King's Cross (later a cinema but now pulled down), and of course I was thrilled to be engaged for a professional appearance while I was still in my last term as a student at the Academy. Claude Rains led the cast, acting three different parts with his usual versatility, and when the play failed after only a few weeks, Playfair kept me on to appear in John

Drinkwater's *Robert E. Lee.* In this play I was to be Lee's aide-de-camp—a very small part in which I had to follow Felix Aylmer about the stage, gazing through my field glasses at a good many rows of empty seats through several weeks of a hot summer, and tripping over my sabre in a long military overcoat. I also understudied Rains, who was playing the juvenile lead in the play, and took over from him for a few performances, gaining some confidence from the ordeal, though I imagine I was merely giving a tentative copy of the way I thought he played the part.

But though he won praise from the critics for several years in plays of many different kinds, Rains never achieved a big star position in London. He finally left England to follow a long and distinguished career on Broadway and afterwards in Hollywood, where his first success was, somewhat ironically, as The Invisible Man. "I can't eat my notices," he once said to me rather sadly, just before he went away. He acted with striking virtuosity and the London stage suffered a great loss when he deserted it for ever.

13

REMARKABLE HOSTESSES

LADY COLEFAX AND LADY CUNARD

I doubt if either of these two ladies would have been pleased to see their names bracketed together during their lifetime, for they were rivals in similar fields. Although they visited each other's houses and knew a great number of the same people, they were not at all similar in character. Some of their guests may have been inclined to be malicious at their expense, but few refused their invitations. Both of them collected lions, political, literary, and theatrical. Both had beautiful houses, and great taste in arranging their rooms, were experts at mixing the various celebrities they entertained, and adept at sparking off lively conversation.

LADY COLEFAX

It was said that Sibyl Colefax had founded her career as a successful hostess by inviting H. G. Wells and Bernard Shaw (on postcards) separately, declaring that each was eager to make the acquaintance of the other. At any rate she soon achieved a great reputation as a party-giver. She lived for many years at Argyll House, Chelsea, next door to another of her social rivals, Mrs. Somerset Maugham, herself an energetic and talented hostess, destined in later years to compete with Lady Colefax as a professional decorator.

The panelled rooms at Argyll House were deliciously scented, and all the latest books—novels, biographies, and poetry—were heaped on a big low table in the drawing-room. There were always beautiful flowers, and the food and drink were perfect without the least display of ostentation. Lady Colefax was a small woman, though not as small as Lady Cunard, who resembled a brilliant canary, with curiously chiselled pale blue eyes. Both ladies were restless and indefatigable. Lady Colefax would think nothing of spending a weekend in the Isle of Wight, driving from Southampton next morning to lunch in Essex, before returning to London to give a party in the evening of the same day. Her car was always full of new books and stationery, so that she could keep abreast of her reading, or scrawl letters and postcards to her friends, both in England and America, in her almost illegible handwriting.

When she first invited me to supper at Argyll House I was naturally impressed to meet so many well-known people, most of whom I had only known before from their photographs in the newspapers. Gertrude Lawrence was to be an important guest on this occasion, but she was very late in arriving, and we sat down to supper without her. At last she was announced, and appeared in the doorway, looking as glamorous as she did on the stage. As she greeted Lady Colefax, she glanced round the supper table, and, seeing a young man seated on my left, sank to the ground in a deep curtsy, thinking him to be the Duke of Kent. Unfortunately he turned out to be a columnist from the *Daily Express,* but neither Lady Colefax or Miss

Lawrence turned a hair. I only went once or twice to Argyll House, as Lady Colefax could no longer afford to live there, and she moved to Lord North Street, Westminster, just before the war, to a much smaller but equally charming house, and opened her decorating business in Brook Street with John Fowler as her partner. However, she still continued to entertain with undiminished enthusiasm all through the war and for some years afterwards, when I grew to know her more intimately and became extremely fond of her. During the long painful illness which finally led to her death she stubbornly refused to give up her love of parties, and I found myself one day lunching in her dining room with a group of ten people, though she herself lay ill upstairs, and we were each of us asked to spend a few minutes with her before we left the house. She was faithfully looked after to the end by the two maids who had been with her for many years and ministered to her and to her guests with unfailing tact and sweetness. Only a few weeks before she died I had met her, walking with a stick and sadly bowed, in the beautiful white garden at Sissinghurst Castle where she was staying with Harold Nicolson and his wife, Vita Sackville-West. We sat down to a big schoolroom tea before we left, with buns and cake and bread and butter—Nicolson (wearing a big straw hat with the brim turned down all round) at one end of the table, and his wife, in boots and breeches, presiding at the other with a large brown teapot in her hand.

LADY CUNARD

Her real christian name was Maud, but she disliked it and was always known as Emerald, though I never heard people call her so to her face. She was American, but soon became an

important figure in London, though she had hunted in Leices-
tershire when she first came to live in England with her rich
husband, Bache Cunard. Her two most intimate and famous
friends were George Moore and Sir Thomas Beecham. She
was extremely intelligent, amusing, and elegant, as well as
being forthright and eagerly inquisitive. She liked to refer to
homosexuals as "popinjays," and delighted to fling challeng-
ing remarks at her guests on every kind of topic as she sat at
the head of her table. She had spent large sums of money as a
patroness of opera and ballet seasons at Covent Garden and
Drury Lane before the First War, and one always met musicians and dancers, as well as writers and politicians, at her
parties. Until the Second War she lived in a large house in
Grosvenor Square, but I only went there once or twice. She
sold the house and went back to America, returning in 1944,
when she established herself in a suite at the Dorchester
Hotel, where she continued to live until her death, surrounded
by her own beautiful impressionist pictures, books, and furniture. During this period I dined with her there a number of
times, and often took her to the theatre, of which she was
passionately fond, when I was not working myself. We would
go by taxi through the blackout to the Chantecler Theatre
near Gloucester Road, where Peter Brook was directing his
first productions in London of Cocteau's *Infernal Machine*
and Ibsen's *John Gabriel Borkman,* and I once spent an
evening with her sitting on a very hard uncomfortable pew at
a church off Regent Street, watching a semi-professional performance of *Everyman.* She slept very little and read vora-
ciously, Greek and Latin classics and poetry as well as contemporary books. She was always punctual and had beautiful
manners. Her coquetry had something of the eighteenth century about it, and she entered or left a room with a brisk
authority that reminded me of Marie Tempest.

I cherish one of her best remarks, an example of what we used to refer to, in a vanishing age of class distinction, as "tumbril talk." It was at one of her supper parties at the Dorchester. The waiter looked rather sulky at being kept up late, though it was only about half-past nine. Lady Cunard had been, as usual, to the theatre, and had invited nine or ten people to join her afterwards. It was the time of the V-2s, which everybody pretended to ignore, though it was impossible not to notice their whining as they went over. It was remarkable how audiences (and actors too) refused to allow the noise to interfere with performances in the theatres. As we sat down Lady Cunard gave a glance round the table and called the Head waiter to her side. "Where is the butter?" she demanded. "Butter, my lady," said the man. "I'm afraid there is no butter." "No butter?" said Lady Cunard. "One must have butter. What is the Merchant Navy doing?" At that moment a V-2 exploded on the other side of the park with a hideous crash, but Lady Cunard did not even appear to have heard it.

I should like to have been able to write something of two other distinguished patronesses of the Arts, but I can only claim a very slight acquaintance with either of them. After the First World War, my eldest brother Lewis went back to Magdalen College, Oxford, invalided from the army. One of his greatest friends, from their earlier Eton days, was Aldous Huxley, whose successful novel *Crome Yellow* made such a great sensation when it was first published. One of the principal characters in this book was drawn from Lady Ottoline Morell, who then lived at a house called Garsington, near Oxford, which my brother told me he had visited with Huxley. There Lady Ottoline held court with an imposing number of writers, painters, and poets whom she delighted to encourage.

She also drove about the country in a yellow phaeton. In 1930 I was acting at Sadler's Wells in a repertoire of Shakespeare plays. Lilian Baylis had only just re-opened the rebuilt theatre, where we played alternate weeks with the Old Vic in Waterloo Road, but business at the Wells was very disappointing. A tall, distinguished, but eccentric-looking lady was always conspicuous at our Saturday matinées. One could hardly fail to notice her long nose and strange horselike face, and the large brown velvet hat that she wore, like a chocolate soufflé, as she sat conspicuously among the many rows of empty seats. One day I was flattered to receive a charming note from her inviting me to tea at her house in Gower Street. With some trepidation I accepted, and found several fascinating celebrities, including Lowes Dickinson and H. G. Wells. Lady Ottoline's house, with a fine portrait of her on the staircase by Augustus John, was as individual as her strange clothes and aristocratic bearing, and that single occasion on which I was her guest made a great impression on me.

Lady Oxford was another eccentric figure whom I met on one or two occasions. I had first noticed her at a private view of the Royal Academy Summer Exhibition, to which I used to be taken by my father when I was quite a small boy. She was then still Mrs. Asquith, whose outspoken and somewhat scandalous memoirs had created a furore. As I watched her rushing about the galleries, in a feathered hat, with her hooked nose and raucous voice, I thought she resembled some maliciously hovering raven. During the Second War she lived at the Savoy Hotel, where I would pass her sitting rather disconsolately in the Grill Room, and she came to a party one night at the Apollo Theatre to celebrate the success of one of Terence Rattigan's war plays, *Flare Path,* which had been directed by her son Anthony. Here I found her in a deserted corner of the bar (where the party was being held) hunched in a low basket chair, mournfully chattering to Henry Irving. But my favourite story (told me by Frederick Ashton) is of her standing defiantly in the hall at the reception given for some smart society wedding, muttering to the guests as they arrived, "Don't go upstairs. The bride's hideous."

14

MUSIC HALLS

I was never a great one for music halls. I much preferred going to plays, and I never cared for animal acts, conjurors, ventriloquists, or clowns. Even the great Grock failed to amuse me, because he was always pretending to play the piano and never did. This trick with a musical instrument has never failed to irritate me, even with such brilliant virtuoso performers as Jack Benny and Victor Borge.

In the Twenties the Halls were beginning to go downhill. The Tivoli closed in 1914, to be later rebuilt as a cinema. Already the Alhambra and the Empire, their famous promenades abolished, alternated variety bills with seasons of revue, ballet, and occasional straight plays and musical comedies. But the Chelsea Palace, the Palladium, the New Oxford, the Kilburn Empire, the Canterbury, and the Metropolitan in Edgware Road, still presented many of the great music-hall stars with a supporting programme of individual turns. The

Hippodromes and Empires in the big provincial cities began to lose their audiences, and American bands and American star performers were hastily engaged to try to revive their popularity, as Danny Kaye and Judy Garland were to do so successfully twenty years later.

However I became a great follower of Paul Whiteman and His Band, and greatly admired Nora Bayes and Sophie Tucker when they first appeared in London. I would sometimes follow them from the Palladium to the Empire to see them twice in a single night, these double appearances being quite a usual tradition of the music hall from the old days. Though I was rather snobbish and superior in my attitude, and inclined to scoff at the highbrow critics, who wrote such clever articles maintaining that the great variety stars were far finer artists than straight actors, I feel very grateful now for the opportunities I had of enjoying many of the most accomplished music-hall performers of the time.

I first saw Harry Tate (with Violet Loraine) in a London Hippodrome revue, *Business as Usual.* The scene was the garden of his house, "The Nest, Tooting Bec," and I think "Fortifying the Home" was the name of the sketch. Later at the Coliseum, in "Fishing," he gave a madly surrealist performance (involving the idiotic fat son who always featured with him as well as a very old man) and the sketch ended with a lot of property fish, of every shape and size, whizzing about in the air on twanging fishing rods as the curtain fell. Will Hay, with his recalcitrant schoolboy class, was another favourite of mine, and the Boganny Brothers, who did a riotous sketch involving pie-throwing. There were usually some ambitious musical interludes in the respectable Coliseum programmes, Mark Hambourg playing Liszt, and a turn entitled "Pattman and his Gigantic Organ" a title which much appealed to my schoolboy sense of humour. "Olga, Elga, and Eli

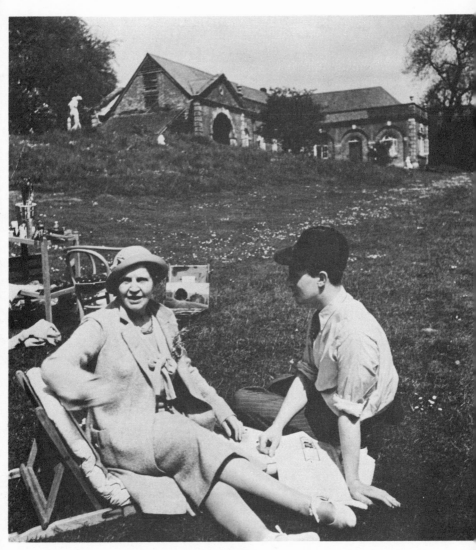

Lady Colefax with Rex Whistler at Ashcombe, *c.* 1937

Rex Whistler, young, handsome, witty, and immensely talented, was one of the most tragic losses sustained by the English theatre. He designed two superb productions: *Pride and Prejudice* and *Victoria Regina* for Gilbert Miller, as well as a number of other plays and ballets, and was an enchanting illustrator of books and posters. His last work was for my production of Congreve's *Love for Love* in 1943, for which he conceived two beautiful scenes, one of them decorated with a Thornhill mural; and his witty designs in the restaurant of the Tate Gallery in Millbank London, entitled *A Search for Rare Meats,* may still be seen there.

When World War Two broke out, he insisted on joining the Guards as a private soldier, soon gained a commission after intensive training, and was an enormously popular officer, delighting his Army friends, with caricatures and wall decorations which he would draw or paint wherever his regiment was quartered.

He was killed on D Day, shot as he was driving in a tank from the Normandy beaches. After the war the city of Brighton was offered his last picture, originally painted on a wall of the room in the Brighton house where he had been billeted just before he left for France.

The Mayor of Brighton assembled with a select group of local worthies to receive the picture with due solemnity, but were greatly put out to discover it was a witty cartoon impersonating the Prince Regent awaking the Spirit of Brighton—a completely nude lady reclining on one arm, while the Prince, coyly bending over her, was also completely naked save for his chestnut wig, the ribbon of the Order of the Garter slung over one shoulder and the Garter itself around his leg, high-heeled shoes, and and only a wisp of chiffon floating about his ample loins.

The picture was (and still is) shown in the Museum adjoining the Brighton Pavilion, but during the first few years after it was accepted, it was kept separately in a small room and an extra charge demanded from anyone who wished to look at it. How Rex would have relished the episode.

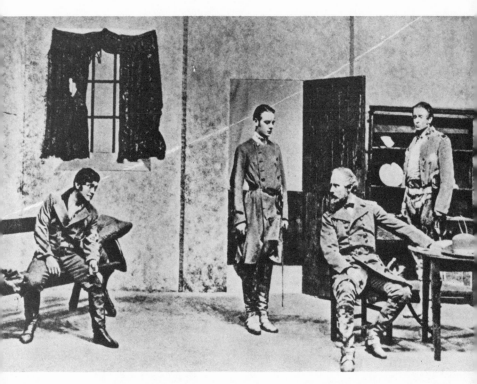

Claude Rains, John Gielgud, Felix Aylmer, and Tristan Rawson in
Robert E. Lee at the Regent Theatre, Kings Cross, 1923

Henry Ainley was a striking young actor (discovered by Benson when
Ainley was a clerk in a Yorkshire bank) and trained in Benson's famous
Shakespearean repertory company, from which a number of players
graduated to London after touring England and playing summer seasons
at Stratford-on-Avon for several years. Under the direction of Harley
Granville-Barker, Ainley later made great successes as Malvolio and
Laertes, and in an adaptation of a novel by Arnold Bennett *The Great
Adventure*. He also played Paolo for George Alexander in a romantic
melodrama *Paolo and Francesca* by Stephen Phillips which was greatly
praised in its time. In the Twenties Ainley went into management at the
St. James's Theatre and presented a number of plays—among others
Redemption—an adaptation of Tolstoy's *The Living Corpse*—and

Shakespeare's *Julius Caesar* in both of which Claude Rains, in supporting parts, won considerable critical success.

Ainley then decided to produce *The Jest*—an adaptation from the Italian of a costume melodrama about two rival brothers which had been a sensational success in New York with John and Lionel Barrymore. During the provincial tour, however, Ainley decided that his part of the elder and brutal brother was less effective, than that played by Rains, the John Barrymore role of an effete romantic and Ainley abandoned the whole project and never brougth the play to London, but it was given many years afterwards when I saw it, re-entitled *The Love Thief* with Norman McKinnel, Ernest Thesiger, and Cathleen Nesbitt in the three leading parts, but achieved no success and ran only a few weeks. This disappointment was felt very deeply by Claude Rains and may have influenced his decision to leave England not many years afterward.

Hudson" used to give an extremely elegant presentation, appearing in full evening dress in the smartest drawing-room interior which the Coliseum could provide, with polar bear skin rugs, brocaded sofas, and tasselled lampshades. In these imposing surroundings they obliged by playing various instruments and singing popular ballads.

George Robey was often to be seen in revues and pantomimes, but his solo turn at a music hall was on the whole more satisfactory, since he had the stage to himself and there was no need for him to pretend to defer to a partner or to try to disguise his unique personality with wigs, make-up, and characterizations. Of course he had invented his own individual get-up—the collarless long frock-coat, the big boots, and huge circular painted eyebrows. Will Fyffe and G. S. Melvin, on the other hand, excelled at mimicry and strange transformations of appearance, and I was never sure whether I would recognize them from one number to the next.

There were few funny women. Beatrice Lillie and Cicely Courtneidge had only just begun to appear as great clowns in the revues which were becoming so popular, and Gracie Fields was touring in a revue *Mr. Tower of London* with her first husband, Archie Pitt, and had not yet taken the West End by storm. But there were a few clever women mimics—Marie Dainton, for instance, and later Elizabeth Pollock and Florence Desmond, rivalled the brilliant mimics Nelson Keys and Robert Hale. The Houston sisters were a fairly broad comedy act (boy and girl) but were also rather dainty. Once I was actually on the bill with them myself at the Coliseum, where there was often one sketch or scene from the straight theatre in the programme. I had been acting as Romeo to Gwen Ffrangcon-Davies's Juliet at the Regent Theatre, King's Cross, and Oswald Stoll suddenly offered us quite a large salary to perform the Balcony Scene for two weeks at the Coliseum after the Regent run had ended. Preceding us in the bill was Teddy Brown, a giant who must have weighed at least twenty stone and played the xylophone with great dexterity. As the revolving stage began to turn in order to allow our setting (an elaborate old-fashioned painted Italian garden) to be wheeled into place, the house was still loudly demanding an encore from Teddy Brown. This, needless to say, did little to increase our confidence, and I was straining every muscle in my upturned neck as I yearned toward the balcony, where Juliet, her red Botticelli wig clashing unhappily with the painted pink marble canvas balustrade on which she leaned, murmured, "Romeo, Romeo, Wherefore art thou Romeo?" We were neither of us very sorry when the curtain fell ten minutes later to very mild applause, though of course we laboured (twice nightly) to become gradually more accustomed to the acoustics of the enormous theatre—no microphones of course in those days—and we felt we had begun to be a little more relaxed by the end of the second week of our engagement. One of the stage hands even took the trouble to tell me at the last performance that in his opinion we had much improved.

It was rather lonely in my big dressing-room behind the scenes, but I used to enjoy standing in the wings to watch the other turns. One man, a German who appeared under the name of Robbins, gave a fascinating performance without speaking a single word. He made strange noises, whispering, humming, and squeaking to himself, changing his costume all the while in front of the audience. He was dressed in layers of strange garments which he kept changing one by one—waistcoats, gloves, braces, trousers, belts. Everything he wore seemed to melt away and turn into something else. And of course from the side I could enjoy watching the way he concealed the garments he had discarded and managed the

trick strings and fastenings which he manipulated so cleverly.
It must have been a tremendous business sorting everything
out and dressing up again in the right order for the next performance. I made friends in those weeks with Billie and
Renée Houston, whose turn used to follow our Balcony
Scene, and the audience would roar as Billie greeted her sister
in her strong Scots accent with, "A thousand times good
night."

I was in front at the Coliseum more often than at any
other variety house, and saw many great stage players there
in scenes and sketches, as well as a large number of variety
stars such as Vesta Tilley, Albert Chevalier, and Little Tich.
Seymour Hicks, Violet or Irene Vanbrugh would sometimes
be the top of the bill, to say nothing of Sarah Bernhardt
("Between tigers, not!" Bernhardt is said to have cabled to
Stoll when he first approached her), and Ellen Terry best of
all. Bernhardt, as old woman with one leg amputated, lay,
half-covered with a cloak, at the foot of a tree as a wounded
poilu in a patriotic one-act play, but I quite believed in her
youthfulness and thrilled to the tones of the famous *voix
d'or,* even though she was reciting words that I could not
understand. And Ellen Terry, as Portia in the Trial Scene,
and as Mistress Page in some excerpts from the *Merry Wives,*
enchanted me to the exclusion of everything else in the programme.

The turns at the Coliseum were always clearly announced
by large illuminated numbers which were shown in frames at
either side of the proscenium. These numbers, though in strict
order on the printed programmes, were apt to vary at different performances. The star turn was supposed always to appear just after the interval, but when Gwen and I gave our
first performance we found we had been shifted to an earlier
less-important place. Only after a day or two did we discover

that it was customary to send five pounds to the stage manager if we wished to hold the top position in which we were billed. During the one long interval the enormous act drop would be lowered, and when I was in front I delighted in spotting the celebrities painted in a great procession on it by Byam Shaw. I found I remembered the details of the curtain very well when I found the original painting for it in a bar at the Coliseum only the other day—Ellen Terry as Beatrice kissing a mittened hand, Bernhardt as L'Aiglon, Tree as Cardinal Wolsey, John Hare, the Vanbrughs, and at least fifty other stage celebrities and opera stars of the period as well.

I only went once to the Kilburn Empire, where I was lucky enough to see Marie Lloyd shortly before she died. She wore a smart Empire dress for her first appearance, with a high diamond-topped ebony stick and some kind of elaborate headdress with aigrettes, and sang, "If you show the boys just a little bit, it's the little bit the boys admire," following this with her famous charwoman number about "The old cock linnet." With birdcage in hand, she sank on to a park bench with very wide slats, remarking, "Oh dear, I'm nipped in the bud."

I never went to the Empire in Leicester Square in the days when the famous promenade permitted the "Pretty Ladies" (as Arnold Bennett called them) to circulate and ply for custom. But after the 1914 War I often went there to enjoy all kinds of different attractions. The Astaires—Fred and Adele—in *Lady, Be Good!;* George Graves and Ethel Levey in *Watch Your Step,* the first revue I ever saw ("You've been eating peas—you're rattling" he said as he put his arm round her waist). In more serious contrast was the Casson-Thorndike production of Shakespeare's *Henry the Eighth* (in which I was surprised to see each character come before

the curtain to take a call—Buckingham, Wolsey, Katherine—
just after they had each played a death-scene) and a spectacular failure, *Arlequin,* with Godfrey Tearle, a romantic-
fantasy with an elaborate Venetian setting.

The Alhambra, too, with its twin domes and imitation
Moorish architecture ornamenting Leicester Square, had a
chequered career from the time of its two great First War-
time revues, *The Bing Boys* and *The Bing Boys on Broadway.* Beatrice Lillie—in top hat and tails—made one of her
first successes in London there in a revue, *5064 Gerrard,* and
much later, just before the theatre was pulled down (to be
rebuilt as the Odeon Cinema) a Shakespeare season was given
there by Stanley Bell, including *Henry V* and *The Merchant
of Venice.* But the Diaghilev seasons from 1919 till the early
Twenties were the great events for me. My father took me to
see *Boutique Fantasque* which had just been produced, with
Massine and Lydia Lopokova and Karsavina still dancing
with the company, while *Carnaval* and *Prince Igor* made up
the rest of the programme. Later the company moved to the
Coliseum where they would give one ballet at each variety
performance, and there I fell madly in love with Tchernicheva, who appeared as the Swan Princess in *Children's
Tale,* and *Thamar* with its towering scenery. I would play
truant from school (Westminster), and Arnold Haskell and
I would climb to the Coliseum gallery, both of us still in our
top hats (rubbed to an effect of wet sealskin by constant
use), and jam pot collars, to see *Petrouchka, Les Matelots*
with Lifar, *Le Train Bleu* with Dolin, and of course *Les
Sylphides. The Good-Humoured Ladies* and *Les Biches, Cleopatra* and *Scheherazade,* thrilled me in another Ballet Season
at the Princes Theatre (now the Shaftesbury) given with
orchestral interludes by Arthur Bliss and Stravinsky.

In 1921 came the great all star revival of *The Sleeping
Princess* at the Alhambra, and I was present on the opening

night, entranced by the splendours of the Bakst décor and brilliant cast—Olga Spessivitzeva as Aurora, Pierre Vladimiroff as the Prince, Idzikowsky, Woizikowsky, Sokolova, Tchernicheva, and Lopokova. But various disasters occurred to spoil the evening's complete success. The magic wood refused to grow, and Lopokova as the Lilac Fairy kept dancing to and fro along the front of the stage waving her wand, while ominous creakings and crackings almost drowned the orchestra. Pieces of wood emerged from the trap only to break off or keel over after they had risen only a few inches from the floor, and the curtain had to be lowered to cover the confusion, while in the final scene one of the dancers fell on her back during a *pas de deux*.

I went to see the ballet many times during its short run. In the end it lost a great deal of money, and Diaghilev was forced to take the company abroad and leave most of the scenery and dresses behind to cover some of his debt to Stoll, though he did manage to salvage the décor of the last act which he used for many years afterwards in *Aurora's Wedding*. The principals in the original Alhambra production varied on different nights, and I saw three other Auroras— Lopokova, Egorova, and Trefilova. Maria D'Albaicin, a beautiful Spaniard, was carried on in a sedan chair (ivory picked out with blue and green) to dance a slow solo variation with castanets, but *The Three Ivans* and *The Blue Bird* were perhaps the most popular items in the final Wedding scene. The King and Queen presided, though they did not dance, sitting on their thrones in tremendous grandeur, surrounded by Negro attendants in magnificent Bakst uniforms. Years afterwards I was lucky enough to meet Stravinsky and his wife in New York, and recognized Mrs. Stravinsky, to her great delight, as that impressive lady on the throne whose beauty I could never forget.

15

DOWN TO EARTH

It is impossible, of course, to award points to an actor or an actress as one might to a horse or a dog, a runner or a cricketer—so many marks for technical ability, so many for timing, characterization, emotional power. The subtleties of the actor's craft are almost impossible to dissect in general terms, and any attempts to examine them in detail, except with the experienced pen of a perceptive professional writer, are apt to prove tedious and unsatisfactory to the average reader. Had I not become an actor myself, I should never have wanted to spoil my enjoyment of the theatre as a member of the audience by speculating on who should receive the final credit for an outstanding performance—author, actor, or director.

In recent years it has sometimes been suggested that rehearsals of a new play should be open to students, members of the audience, and even to the dramatic critics. I believe I speak for most of my colleagues in thinking that such a procedure would be an intolerable intrusion on the privacy of our work. Already we are bound to complete our experiments by a fixed deadline, hoping to be prepared in time, but the first performance we give in public is often greatly inferior, as we ourselves well know, to the result we can achieve after playing before an audience for several weeks. Hence the modern custom of try-outs, sometimes for more than a month, before we venture to appear in London.

In my young days first nights in the West End were apt to be extremely ragged. The prompter's voice was often much in evidence, and lighting, scene changes, and stage management were apt to go astray. This atmosphere of uncertainty, though the audience might accept it as part of the excitement of launching a new production, must have played more than usual havoc with the nerves of the players, especially in the case of the star of the company who was frequently the manager and director as well.

One evening last summer I was invited to give a talk about the theatre to a group of American students who were on a visit to London, and when, at the end, I asked for questions, a young man with a beard jumped up and demanded in rather threatening tones, "What, in your opinion, is a star?" I circumvented him with a fairly non-committal answer, remembering too late that, when Ralph Richardson and I had been interviewed on television in America by David Frost, he had asked the same question, and Ralph had swiftly countered him by answering firmly, "Ethel Merman."

Was I deceived as a schoolboy into thinking that every actor or actress whose name appeared in big type was a blazing genius? Though I was lucky enough to see three great actresses, Bernhardt, Duse, and Ellen Terry, the aura of devotion which surrounded them, even in their decline, impressed me so greatly that I could not possibly, at that early age, attempt to compare their qualities or discriminate between their respective talents. I could only marvel at their staying-power and the mystique which still clung to them to the very end of their long careers. In my youth I was a wonderfully appreciative member of the audience—less so, alas, today. Though of course I imagined myself to be highly critical I suppose I was easily taken in by claptrap. But I do remember saying once, "I wish I could have a photograph of Edith Evans. I can never recognize her when she comes on to the stage. She always looks exactly like the part she is playing." I suppose this was really the greatest compliment I could have paid her. Of course I developed my own personal likes and dislikes and was prepared to voice them in no uncertain terms, and I did begin to realize, even when I was quite young, the difficulty that must beset a critic if he finds the mannerisms of some popular player particularly irritating or unattractive.

What is it that makes the so-called "star"? Energy, an athletic voice, a well-graced manner, certainty of execution, some unusually fascinating originality of temperament? Vitality, certainly, and the ability to convey an impression of beauty or ugliness as the part demands, as well as authority and a sense of style.

The actor's loyalty to the playwright has certainly grown steadily during my time. In the early years of the century, Vedrenne and Barker had laboured to create good ensemble companies, and to accustom the public to appreciate them, rather than the bravura vehicles of the Victorian and Edwardian theatre, but their ventures were considered highbrow and were not really popular with the general public. Barker's Shakespeare productions at the Savoy between 1912–14 were considered stunty and *avant-garde,* and even Shaw's plays (except for *Pygmalion* and *Arms and the Man*) appealed to a very limited audience for many years after they were written. I saw a number of them for the first time when they were given for short seasons after the Great War at the tiny Everyman Theatre in Hampstead, with splendid casts—Nicholas Hannen, Claude Rains, Edith Evans, and many other distinguished players. But *Saint Joan* was surely the first of Shaw's plays to be a big popular success.

The old-fashioned theatre manners died hard—the divisions of class in the audience, evening dress in stalls and boxes, late-comers banging down their seats, booing from the gallery if the patrons were disappointed, incidental music, receptions for the leading players, and curtain calls after every act. (Even up to 1933 this custom still prevailed and we took several bows after each act of *Richard of Bordeaux*.) Some of the artificial excitement generated by all this sense of occasion was, of course, undoubtedly genuine, and helped to make a visit to the theatre a treat for young people and a privileged hobby for the older enthusiasts, who looked upon it as a regular social event at which they were sure to meet their friends, and could discuss the play with them in the intervals, and at each other's dinner parties in the weeks that followed.

Now of course everything is changed. Men sit in the stalls in their shirt-sleeves with their arms round the necks of their companions. They take off their shoes and put their feet up on the ledges of the boxes. But radio and television have made audiences, on the whole, more intelligently curious and better informed than they used to be, and they tend to be far more punctual as well as more attentive. If they are inclined to read newspapers while they are waiting for the play to start, their behaviour may be justified by the fact that there is now no overture to arouse their expectation, with the lights half-lowered and the footlights glowing, and the curtain is often already up when they come into the theatre. This is one of the strange new obsessions of modern directors that I have never been able to bring myself to like, though of course it is impossible to avoid it on an open stage, but in a proscenium theatre I find it a greatly disenchanting beginning to the evening.

Plays used to be clearly differentiated, and people knew just the kind of thing they wished to see, as well as the actual theatre where they were most likely to find it. Nowadays the agents and coach-parties direct their mass of patrons to a "good show," promising either wholesome family fun or a few less savoury dishes for the stag-line. Melodrama is scarce, since it can be more richly effective in the cinema, but thrillers still seem to have their old appeal. The serious theatre, with its three main centres, the National, the Royal Shakespeare at the Aldwych, and the English Stage Company at the Court, supply rich and varied programmes, both classical and contemporary, and so do the smaller experimental houses in various parts of London. Television creates new stars. Some of them may have struggled without conspicuous success for many years in the theatre, now to be suddenly taken to the hearts of an enormous audience who might never otherwise have noticed them. The danger of this sudden success is, of course, in overexposure, a danger equally great in the world of films and pop singing.

In the old days, the great music-hall comedians lived on the same material for their whole lives. Even if they had new songs written for them over the years, the tunes and lyrics were derived much in the same style as the old ones in which they had made their first successes. But television, radio, and piped music tend to exhaust every successful tune in a very few weeks for a larger audience than was ever imagined before, and the resulting competition has created a new world of agents and teams of gag-writers, with frenzied efforts to find new kinds of presentation, often of an abstract and surrealistic kind, which can quickly exhaust their ephemeral popularity.

How often in the past has the theatre been said to be in its last throes, yet it obstinately continues to survive. The changes that have transformed it in all its branches, especially in the last twenty years, have been violent and sudden, and it is often difficult for one to appreciate and understand them as one grows older. But I believe that there are as many great personalities today as there were in the theatre fifty years ago, and that on the whole they are considerably more generous and less selfish people than many of their predecessors used to be.

But the star of today has a very difficult task in trying to maintain some mystery, and yet to behave naturally and with some sort of modesty at the same time. The tape-recorder and the television camera can take his voice, his manner, and his face into millions of homes, while candid cameras and newshounds dog his private life when he is off the stage. But there is no doubt that the public still loves to worship actors and actresses whose personalities are strikingly original, sympathetic, or unusual, and the young adore their stage idols as well as their musical film favourites and pop singers, just as we all did in our own early theatre-going days so many years ago.

INDEX

Acis and Galatea, 37
Advise and Consent, 127
Agate, James, 54
Alexander, Sir George, 12, 80, 91
Alibi, 127
Alice Sit by the Fire, 21, 82, 110
Ambrose Applejohn's Adventure, 81
Anderson, Dame Judith, 64, 67, 69
Andrews, Harry, 67, 103
And So to Bed, 114, 115
Anna Christie, 66
Antigone, 70
Apple Cart, The, 123
Arden, Jane, 126
Aria, Mrs., 7
Aristocrat, The, 91
Arlequin, 161
Arms and the Man, 137
Armstrong, John, 127
Arnaud, Yvonne, 59, 107, 114, 115
Arsenic and Old Lace, 58
Asche, Oscar, 8
Astaire, Adele and Fred, 160
Atwood, Clare, 34, 36
Aunt of England, The, 92
Aurora's Wedding, 162
Aylmer, Felix, 142
Aynesworth, Allan, 78, 79

Back to Methusalah, 123
Baddeley, Hermione, 89
Bancroft, Sir Squire, 11
Banks, Leslie, 89
Barker, Harley Granville-, 102, 168
Barretts of Wimpole Street, The, 124
Barrett, Wilson, 93

Barrie, Sir James M., 100
Barrymore, Ethel, 67
Barrymore, John, 50, 67
Bayes, Nora, 156
Baylis, Lilian, 37, 150
Beach, Sylvia, 41
Beardsley, Aubrey, 49
Beecham, Sir Thomas, 148
Beerbohm, Max, 19, 55, 77
Behold the Bridegroom, 64
Behold We Live, 134
Bells, The, 23
Bennett, Arnold, 91, 160
Benny, Jack, 155
Benson, Sir Frank, 12
Berg, Gertrude, 124
Bernhardt, Sarah, 52, 141, 159
Bernstein, Sidney, 37
Bing Boys on Broadway, The, 7, 161
Bing Boys, The, 161
Bledsoe, Jules, 64
Blue Bird, The, 162
Borge, Victor, 155
Bourchier, Arthur, 12, 13
Boutique Fantasque, 161
Boyer, Charles, 126
Braithwaite, Dame Lilian, 20, 57
Brandeis University, 69
Brayton, Lily, 8, 11
Breadwinner, The, 82
Brookfield, Charles, 80
Brook, Peter, 149
Brough, Mary, 114
Brown, Teddy, 158
Browne, Graham, 111
Brynner, Yul, 134

Bulldog Drummond, 78
Burton, Richard, 82
Business as Usual, 157
Butt, Alfred, 11
By Candle Light, 59, 82, 115, 121
Byng, Douglas, 101
Byron, Arthur, 67

Cadell, Jean, 81
Caesar and Cleopatra, 102
Café Royal, 7, 37
Campbell, Stella Beatrice (Mrs. Patrick), 24, 46, 48, 49, 99, 102, 122, 138
Captain Brassbound's Conversion, 21, 59
Carnaval, 161
Carousel, 126
Casson, Sir Lewis, 87, 103
Cenci, The, 103
Cherry Orchard, The, 82, 124, 125, 127
Chevalier, Albert, 159
Children's Tale, The, 161
Chiltern Hundreds, 83
Chu Chin Chow, 9, 11
Circle, The, 80
Clare, Mary, 89
Clark, Holman, 4
Clarkson, Willie, 7
Cleopatra, 71, 161
Cochran, C. B., 37
Cochrane, Frank, 8
Colefax, Sibyl (Lady), 146, 147
Collins, Arthur, 13
Compton, Fay, 35, 66, 67, 126, 137
Constant Nymph, The, 26
Cooper, Dame Gladys, 35, 81
Coquette, 63
Courtneidge, Dame Cicely, 158
Coward, Sir Noël, 20, 46, 54, 66, 89, 110, 133, 134, 141
Cowl, Jane, 66
Craig, Edith Gordon, 32, 33, 34, 35, 36, 37

Craig, Edward Gordon, 21, 23, 31, 33, 37, 38, 40, 41
Craig, Nellie, 40
Crome Yellow, 149
Cukor, George, 67
Cunard, Maud (Emerald, Lady), 145, 148, 149–50
Cymbeline, 103
Cyrano de Bergerac, 89, 91, 140

Dainton, Marie, 158
D'Alverez, Marguerite, 49
Daniel, 141
Dark Lady of the Sonnets, The, 91
Dead Heart, The, 22
Dean, Basil, 27, 87
Dear Brutus, 78
Dear Octopus, 112, 114
de Havilland, Olivia, 82
de la Condamine, Robin. *See* Farquharson, Robert
Dell, Jeffrey, 127
Desmond, Florence, 158
Diaghilev, Serge Pavlovich, 161, 162
Dickinson, Lowes, 150
Dido and Aeneas, 37
Distaff Side, The, 93
Doctor's Dilemma, The, 72, 99, 141
Dodsworth, 68
D'Orme, Aileen, 9
Dorothy o' the Hall, 19
Dover Road, The, 80
Drake, 79
Duel of Angels, 70
Duke of Windsor, 68
Dulac, Edmond, 89
du Maurier, Sir Gerald, 12, 77, 84, 134

Easy Virtue, 66
Ellen Terry and Her Secret Self, 34
Elliott, Gertrude. *See* Forbes-Robertson, Lady
Elsom, Isobel, 103, 142
English Stage Co., 169
Entertainments National Service Association, 58

Evans, Dame Edith, 22, 103, 137, 140, 167, 168
Everyman, 149

Faber, Leslie, 115, 119
Fairbrother, Sydney, 9
Fallen Angels, 134
Farmer's Wife, The, 123
Farquharson, Robert, 97, 102–4
Farren, William, 24
Father, The, 91, 137
Ferber, Edna, 92, 112
Ffrangcon-Davies, Gwen, 99, 102, 124, 158
Fields, Gracie, 158
Finney, Albert, 126
First Mrs. Fraser, The, 112
Fiske, Mrs., 50, 66
5064 Gerrard, 161
Flare Path, 150
Fontanne, Lynn, 69
Forbes-Robertson, Lady, 48, 49
Forster, E. M., 127
Frost, David, 167
Fumed Oak, 134
Furness, Thelma, 133
Fyffe, Will, 158

Gachet, Alice, 126
Galileo, 126
Galsworthy, John, 66, 87
Garbo, Greta, 66
Garland, Judy, 156
Garrick Club, 83
Gay Lord Quex, The, 134
General Post, 58
Geneva, 100
Ghosts, 47, 48, 49
Gielgud, Lewis, 150
Gielgud, Val, 12, 122
Girl in the Taxi, The, 114
Gish, Lillian, 67, 68
Glass Menagerie, The, 66
Godwin, Edward, 32
Good-Humoured Ladies, The, 161
Graves, George, 160
Greet, Clare, 121

Grock, 155
Guthrie, Tyrone, 67, 103, 112, 125, 128
Gwenn, Edmund, 12

Hackett, James, 52, 122
Hackett, Walter, 81
Hale, Robert, 158
Hambourg, Mark, 157
Hamlet, 42, 66, 67, 68, 69, 99
Hampden, Walter, 69
Hands Across the Sea, 134
Hannen, Nicholas, 67, 168
Harding, Lyn, 122
Hardwicke, Sir Cedric, 123, 126
Hare, Sir John, 160
Harvey, Martin, 52
Haskell, Arnold, 161
Havoc, 121
Hawtrey, Sir Charles, 77, 79, 80, 81, 82, 84
Hayes, George, 36
Hayes, Helen, 63, 69
Hay Fever, 109
Hay, Will, 156
Heartbreak House, 123
Hedda Gabler, 47
Henry the Eighth, 89, 103, 160
Henry V, 161
Hervey House, 66, 67
Hicks, Sir Seymour, 159
High Tide on the Lincolnshire Coast, 52
Holt, Maud. *See* Tree, Lady
Home and Beauty, 80
Home, William Douglas, 83
Houston, Billie and Renée, 158, 159
Howard, Leslie, 67, 68
Howard, Sidney, 66
Hudson, Elga, Eli and Olga, 157
Huntersmoon, 122
Huxley, Aldous, 150

Ibsen, Henrik, 46
Ideal Husband, An, 80
If I Were King, 124

Importance of Being Earnest, The,
    79, 82, 128
Indoor Fireworks, 56
Infernal Machine, 148
In Good King Charles's Golden Days,
    100
Insect Play, The, 141
Interference, 78
In the Night, 120
Invisible Man, The, 142
Irving, H. B., 12
Irving, Sir Henry, 7, 32

Jack Straw, 81
Jane Clegg, 121
Jerome, Jerome K., 93
John Gabriel Borkman, 46, 148
Johnson, President Lyndon B., 68
Journey's End, 139
Julius Caesar, 82
Justice, 66

Karsavina, Tamara, 161
Kaye, Danny, 156
Keane, Doris, 21, 50
Keen, Malcolm, 67
Keith-Johnston, Colin, 124
Kelly, Charles, 32
Kendal, (Dame Madge) Mrs., 12,
    20, 111
Kennedy, Margaret, 27
Kennedy, President John, 68
Keys, Nelson, 11, 158
King, Ada, 87, 89, 90
King and I, The, 134
King, Dennis, 69
King Lear, 128
Knoblock, Edward, 91
Komisarjevsky, 37, 126

Lady Be Good, 160
Lady's Not for Burning, The, 8
Lady Windermere's Fan, 20
Lanchester, Elsa, 127
Landi, Elissa, 139
Lang, Matheson, 103, 123

Last of Mrs. Cheyney, The, 82
Laughton, Charles, 103, 125, 126–
    28, 134
Lawrence, Gertrude, 66, 131–34, 147
Lee, Gypsy Rose, 133
Le Gallienne, Eva, 126
Leigh, Vivien, 56, 70
Le Train Bleu, 161
Leighton, Margaret, 125
Les Biches, 161
Les Matelots, 161
Letter, The, 121
Levey, Ethel, 160
Likes of 'Er, The, 89
Liliom, 126
Lillie, Beatrice, 68, 134, 158, 161
Lindsay, Howard, 69
Lister, Francis, 89
Little Catherine, 112
Little Tich, 159
Lloyd, Marie, 160
London Calling, 134
Lopokova, Lydia, 161
Loraine, Robert, 137–40
Loraine, Violet, 7, 157
Lord, Pauline, 66
Louis XI, 23
Love For Love, 51, 115
Lunt, Alfred, 69
Lynn, Ralph, 114

Macbeth, 101, 121, 128
McClintic, Guthrie, 66, 67
McEvoy, Charles, 89
McKinnel, Norman, 58
Macquoid, Percy, 13
Major Barbara, 121, 126
Majority of One, A, 125
Man and Superman, 126, 138
Marsh, Edward, 7
Marsh, Howard, 64
Marshall, Chris, 34
Marshall, Herbert, 89
Mary Rose, 100, 137
Mask of Virtue, 56, 70
Massine, Léonide, 161

Matriarch, The, 47
Matthews, A. E., 77, 79–83
Maugham, Mrs., 146
Maugham, Somerset, 80, 92
Measure for Measure, 125
Men's Dress Reform League, 101
Mercer, Mabel, 64
Merchant of Venice, 22, 161
Merry Wives of Windsor, 20
Michael and His Lost Angel, 49
Milestones, 91
Millard, Evelyn, 13
Mr. Tower of London, 158
Molyneux, Edward, 133
Month in the Country, A, 81
Moore, George, 148
Moorehead, Agnes, 126
Morell, Lady Ottoline, 150
Morgan, Helen, 64
Much Ado About Nothing, 124
Musical Chairs, 27
Mutiny on the Bounty, 125

Nance Oldfield, 21
National Theatre Co., 169
Naughty Wife, The, 81
Nazimova, 66
Neilson, Julia, 13, 17
Neilson-Terry, Phyllis, 122
Nicolson, Harold, 148
Nijinsky, Vaslav, 101
No Man's Land, 93
Norton, Frederic, 9
Novello, Ivor, 53, 126

O'Farrell, Mary, 82
Oliver, Edna May, 63
Olivia, 21
Olivier, Sir Laurence, 40, 70, 112
On Approval, 82
O'Neill, Eugene, 66
On the Art of the Theatre, 37
On the Spot, 127
On With the Dance, 101
Othello, 140
Our Betters, 20

Ouspenskaya, Maria, 68, 69
Outsider, The, 120
Outward Bound, 120
Oxford, Margot, Lady, 150

Party, 126
Passing of the Third Floor Back, 93
Pasture, Mrs. Henry de la, 82
Patriot, The, 66, 103, 123
Payment Deferred, 127
Peg O' My Heart, 82
Pelléas and Mélisande, 52
Percy, Esmé, 36, 56, 97–99
Perkins, Osgood, 66
Peter Pan, 4
Peter's Mother, 82
Petrouchka, 161
Pinero, Sir Arthur Wing, 46
Pitt, Archie, 158
Players Club, 66, 69
Playfair, Arthur, 11
Pollock, Elizabeth, 158
Pounds, Courtice, 9
Prince Igor, 161
*Private Life of Henry the Eighth,
The,* 125
Private Lives, 134
Pygmalion, 47, 49, 99, 138

Queen Was in the Parlour, The, 88

R.U.R., 88
Raffles, 78
Rains Came, The, 68
Rains, Claude, 140, 141, 142
Ravenswood, 23
Redgrave, Sir Michael, 82
Réjane, Gabrielle, 111
Rembrandt, 134
Reynolds, James, 132
Richard of Bordeaux, 168
Richard the Second, 72
Richard the Third, 124
Richardson, Sir Ralph, 124, 166
Ringer, The, 120, 121
Rivals, The, 141

Robert E. Lee, 142
Robey, George, 7, 157
Robson, Dame Flora, 103
Romance, 50
Romeo and Juliet, 26
Roosevelt, President Franklin D., 68
Rorke, Mary, 141
Royal Family, The, 92
Royal Shakespeare Company, 169
Rutherford, Dame Margaret, 67

Sackville-West, Vita, 147
Saint Joan, 100, 168
St. John, Christopher, 36
Saintsbury, H. A., 92
Salome, 102
Salvation, 66
Salvation Nell, 50
Scarlet Pimpernel, The, 23, 24
Scheherazade, 161
Schildkraut, Joseph, 126
Second Mrs. Tanqueray, The, 46
Shakespeare Tercentenary Performance, 12
Shaw, George Bernard, 34, 46, 48, 71, 100, 145
Shaw, Glen Byam, 112, 160
Shaw, Martin, 37
Sheldon, Edward, 50
Shewing-up of Blanco Posnet, 99
Show Boat, 63
Sign of the Cross, 93
Sign on the Door, The, 121
Silver Box, The, 87
Skin of Our Teeth, The, 70, 73
Sleeping Princess, The, 161
Sleeping Prince, The, 70
Smallhythe Farm, 34
Spessivitzeva, Olga, 162
Squire, Ronald, 77, 78, 81, 115, 121
Stanislavsky, 42
Stern, G. B., 47
Stevens, Emily, 66
Stoll, Sir Oswald, 158
Stravinsky, Mrs., 162

Street Car Named Desire, A, 46, 70, 73
Strindberg, August, 91
Such Men Are Dangerous, 102, 122
Sunday Dinner Club, 66
Swinley, Ion, 138, 139
Sylphides, Les, 161

Tate, Harry, 156
Taylor, Laurette, 66, 82
Taylor, Valerie, 81
Tchernicheva, Liubov, 162
Tearle, Sir Godfrey, 161
Tempest, Dame Marie, 8, 58, 59, 92, 107, 108, 114, 116, 148
Tempest, The, 37
Ten Commandments, The, 124
Terris, Norma, 63
Terry, Dame Ellen, 8, 13, 14, 17, 20, 21, 22, 32, 33, 34, 36, 37, 40, 50, 59, 82, 159, 160
Terry, Fred, 13, 17–26
Terry, Marion, 13, 19, 20, 21, 22, 82
Terry, Phyllis, 25
Terry-Lewis, Mabel, 48, 79
Thamar, 161
Theatre Royal, 111
Theatres
  Adlwych, 169
  Alhambra, 7, 155, 161
  Ambassadors, 89, 75
  Borough, Stratford, 27
  Broadhurst, 69
  Canterbury, 155
  Chantecler, 148
  Chelsea Palace, 155
  Coliseum, 156, 159
  Court, 169
  Daly's, 35
  Drury Lane, 111
  Empire, 67, 88, 156
  Everyman, 137, 168
  Gaiety, 87
  Hippodrome, 156
  His Majesty's, 55, 66, 140
  Kilburn Empire, 155

Lyceum, 21, 23
Lyric, Hammersmith, 137
Majestic, 115
Manhatten Opera House, 11
Metropolitan, 155
New, 124
New Oxford, 155
Old Vic, 37, 54, 70, 103
Palace, 11
Palladium, 155
Phoenix, 36
Prince's (Shaftsbury), 161
Queen's, 90, 111, 112
Regent, King's Cross, 141
Sadler's Wells, 103, 150
St. James's, 70, 79
St. Martin's, 89
Shubert, 115
Stratford, 70
Tivoli, 155
Thesiger, Ernest, 97, 99–101, 138
Thomson, Beatrix, 140
Thorndike, Dame Sybil, 35, 87, 103, 120
Thorpe, Courtenay, 7, 102
Three Ivans, The, 162
Three Sisters, The, 126
Tiger Cats, 139
Tilley, Vesta, 159
Titheradge, Madge, 58, 89, 111, 122
Titus Andronicus, 73
Tonight at 8:30, 132
Tons of Money, 114
Tree, Sir Herbert, 11, 45, 54
Tree, Lady, 45, 54, 89, 92
Tree, Viola, 56
Trevelyan, Hilda, 4
Truman, President Harry S, 68
Tucker, Sophie, 156
Tully, George, 58

Unknown, The, 91

Vanity Fair, 11, 111
Vanbrugh, Dame Irene, 8, 159
Vanbrugh, Violet, 8, 101
Venne, Lottie, 81
Vibart, Henry, 141
Victoria Regina, 69, 79
Vikings, The, 20
Vladimiroff, Pierre, 162
Vortex, The, 19, 57, 58

Walkley, A. B., 7
Walls, Tom, 114
Ward, Dame Geneviève, 13, 14, 90
Warner, Charles, 20
Watch Your Step, 160
Waterloo Bridge, 73
Watson, Malcolm, 7
Watts, G. F., 33
Way of the World, The, 137, 139
Way Things Happen, The, 89, 90
Webb, Alan, 67
Welles, Orson, 126
Wells, H. G., 145, 150
Whale, James, 138
Where the Rainbow Ends, 4
White Cargo, 120
Whiteman, Paul, 107
Wilde, Oscar, 80
Will Shakespeare, 91
Williams, Emlyn, 90, 115
Williams, Harcourt, 37
Williams, Tennesee, 66
Winninger, Charles, 64
Winter's Tale, 20
Wolfit, Sir Donald, 23
Woollcott, Alexander, 54
Wright, Haidée, 87, 90–93

Yellow Sands, 123